Never Stand Behind A Loaded Horse

This book belongs to:

Brenda Brett

Never Stand Behind
A Loaded Horse

Gordon Kirkland

thistledown press

National Library of Canada Cataloguing in Publication

Kirkland, Gordon, 1953 –
Never stand behind a loaded horse / Gordon Kirkland.

ISBN 1-894345-72-X

1. Canadian wit and humor (English) 2. Kirkland, Gordon,
1953-
– Anecdotes. I. Title.

PN6178.C3K573 2004   C818'.5402   C2004-900126-4

Cover photographs by Leonard McGregor,
Master of Photographic Arts
Cover and book design by J. Forrie
Typeset by Thisttledown Press

Thistledown Press Ltd.
633 Main Street
Saskatoon, Saskatchewan, S7H 0J8
www.thistledown.sk.ca

Thistledown Press gratefully acknowledges the financial assistance of the
Canada Council for the Arts, the Saskatchewan Arts Board, and the
Government of Canada through the Book Publishing Industry
Development Program for its publishing program.

For Diane, Brad and Mike
who make it all worthwhile,

and, in loving memory of Nipper (1988 – 2001)
the dumbest dog to ever get lost on a single flight of
stairs, who always thought I was right, especially
if I had a piece of pizza in my hand.

Acknowledgements

I have been blessed with good friends, old and new, who have been great sources of encouragement, both with this book, and with my first one, *Justice Is Blind — and Her Dog Just Peed In My Cornflakes* (Harbour Publishing, 1999.) I especially want to thank my friends Blaine and Bretta, Lars and Jan, and Wayne and Peggy, as well as my brother, Jim, and sister, Lois, and their families for the big part they've played in my life while writing this book.

Of course, none of this could have ever been written without the faith and encouragement I receive daily from my best friend Diane who has been my wife through "thickness and health" for the past thirty years. She, along with my sons Brad and Mike, bring life to my stories and stories to my life.

I'd be remiss if I didn't mention a couple of friends who have inspired me over the years.

Lynn Johnston taught me to laugh at the daily humor in marriage, parenting, and dog ownership. She made me see that life really is *For Better Or For Worse* everyday.

Ridley Pearson is the most organized writer I know. With every word he puts on paper, he encourages me to be a better writer.

I am a lucky man to know them both.

And finally I'd need to thank everyone who came out to see me as I toured in both Canada and the United States over the last few years. The audiences, booksellers, reviewers, radio hosts, and television interviewers who supported me really made it a lot of fun. I look forward to doing it all again.

CONTENTS

My Best Friend Is A Dog, She Just Doesn't Know It

Life Is Strange — And I Do My Part To Keep It That Way

INTRODUCTION

Spending many years writing a syndicated humor column helped me develop my writing style, but nothing could have prepared me for the impact of seeing my first book in print.

Justice Is Blind — and Her Dog Just Peed In My Cornflakes hit the stands in April of 1999. I hit the road in May. Over the course of the next six months I did appearances in almost seventy cities in Canada and the United States. That included countless bookstore appearances, guest spots on radio and television, and conference speaking engagements.

I had a secret goal for the book. I wanted to have it nominated for the Stephen Leacock Memorial Medal for Humour, one of the most sought after literary awards in Canada. I received word in late December of 1999 that the book had indeed been nominated, along with forty-eight other books. In March of 2000, I learned that it had been chosen as one of the five finalists. While the book didn't win the Medal, it did take home the Award of Merit, far more than I could have ever fantasized. I owe the Steven Leacock Associates a great debt of gratitude for the honor they bestowed upon me.

This book contains more of the same sort of stories that appeared in the first one. I write about life from the perspective of a husband, married to the same wife for more than thirty years, the father of two sons, and the master of Nipper, the dumbest dog to ever get lost on a single flight of stairs. (Unfortunately Nipper passed away in my arms on Labor Day weekend, 2001. I still miss her.)

My world brings me a constant supply of stories to share with my readers, because there never seems to be a short supply of events and situations that strike me as funny, and for that I am truly thankful. I hope you enjoy reading about them as much as I've enjoyed living through them.

— Gordon Kirkland

PS. On the cover, I'm the one on the left. No, not my left, your left.

For Some Reason People Wonder
How She Puts Up With Me . . .

It sounded like a good idea at the time. But you should always be wary of good sounding ideas that occur to you in the middle of the night, especially when you're 250 miles from home.

My wife and I watched our son play hockey one July night. Yes, I said July. It didn't matter. Brad played hockey twelve months of the year. As a result Diane and I developed a chemical imbalance in our brains, caused by an overexposure to sweaty hockey equipment that makes us willing to sit in an arena in July to watch him play.

Our original plan was to watch his game, which didn't finish until 1:30 AM, thanks to a late start and an overtime period, go back to our campsite for a couple of hours sleep, and then drive home so that Diane could get to her office in the morning.

This was a good plan.

This was a workable plan.

This was a smart plan, which explains why I decided to come up with another plan.

I reasoned that if we drove into the campground at 2:00 AM and then left again at 4:00 AM, we probably wouldn't be very popular with the other campers. I also figured that a twenty-ounce cup of coffee would have enough caffeine to see me through the mountains.

I may have been right on my first assumption, but it didn't take too long to prove that twenty ounces of coffee was completely insufficient. By then we were in the middle of nowhere, far away from the nearest working coffeepot.

Amazing things start to happen when you're driving at a time that you'd really rather be sleeping. I always find that the road gets considerably better. What was once a two-lane highway appears to be a multi-lane freeway. Now that I wear trifocal glasses, I can see as many as twelve additional lanes. This is especially handy when driving through the mountains. With so many lanes to choose from, the odds are pretty good that at least one of them will take you where you want to go without sending you over a cliff.

For some strange reason, Diane was concerned that I might fall asleep at the wheel. This, of course, was just needless worrying on her part. Every time she felt me jerk the car back into the right lane, or heard the tires crossing the lane markers, she'd jump and ask me if I was awake. How could I possibly sleep with her doing that every couple of minutes?

When I really started to feel drowsy, I knew it was time to bring out my old tried-and-true method of staying awake at the wheel. I've used this technique for years and it has never failed to produce startling results. It doesn't involve ingesting any artificial stimulants, and you can repeat it as often as necessary without having to refer to your physician. You might want to try it the next time you find yourself nodding off at 70 miles per hour.

The first step is to open your car window and take in several deep breaths of fresh, cool night air. This, of course, assumes that you are driving somewhere where the air is fresh. It may not be wise to try filling your lungs with the air in some metropolitan areas, near slaughterhouses, or if you are following a truckload of cattle.

The second stage of the process is the most important, and you must be carefully prepared for it, both mentally and physically. With your lungs filled to their maximum capacity with fresh, oxygen-rich air, look straight ahead at the road, open your mouth wide, and scream.

Loudly.

Scream at the top of your lungs for as long as you can without doing irreparable harm to your vocal cords, ears, and/or windshield. The resulting adrenaline rush is incredibly stimulating. You are immediately wide-awake and able to focus on the road with renewed concentration. If you do a really good job, every dog within a five-mile radius will also be wide-awake.

Of course, it's best if you are alone in your car when you do this.

If you are not alone, you should probably warn your companion about what you are about to do. This is especially true if they are already asleep. Having the person in the passenger seat suddenly regain consciousness while you're screaming like a banshee can be dangerous for all concerned. The person is likely to sit bolt upright, flail her arms about wildly, and start speaking in tongues.

At least, that's what Diane did.

Every so often, when I have managed to get on Diane's nerves especially well, she threatens to trade me in on a newer model. She has this idea that she could get two new twenty-five year old sports models for her fifty-year-old rust-bucket.

I think she might have a bit of trouble making that trade. Even if she could find a couple of twenty-five year olds, she probably couldn't trade me in unless they were having one of those push, pull, or drag trade-in sales.

When you trade a car in you have to sign a declaration detailing any accidents it might have been in. That's where my value would be shot. It would be like the time we tried to trade a battered old car on a new one and the dealer offered to take another couple hundred off the price if he didn't have to take our car. Diane could get stuck with her new sports models and still have me taking up most of the room in the garage.

I've had a few accidents since I first hit the road. I've broken my left arm, my left leg, my spine, more ribs than you'd find in Chinese food buffet, and perhaps most spectacularly, my right big toe, but that's another story.

Oh sure, I've been repaired, but some of that damage just stays with you, like it does if you bend the frame on a station wagon. No matter how good the exterior looks or how well the engine runs when you get it back from the shop, it will never perform quite the same.

Some of the damage is pretty obvious. Just looking at me will tell you that I broke my spine. The crutches and wheelchair tend to give it away. That kind of thing is definitely a detriment to trade-in values.

I have my share of the human equivalent to parking lot door dings, too. I have scars that have been there since I was a kid. My finish is getting a bit wrinkled, and my once black hood has faded to a mottled gray. My right big toe has an odd bend to it that's left over from when I broke it so spectacularly in 1965, but again that's another story.

Let's not even discuss my exhaust emissions, Okay?

My engine isn't all that efficient. I give it lots of fuel, and it always seems ready for more, especially the high-test fuels like cheese and chocolate, and it stores most of it around my belly instead of using it to move me around faster.

Whether I'm on my crutches or using my wheelchair, I guess you could say that I have four on the floor. I've never really understood just exactly what that term means. It would seem to put me on par with my cerebrally challenged dog. She has four on the floor too, that is unless she's sleeping on the couch, in which case she has none on the floor.

I have managed to have none on the floor several times, but only for very brief periods. It's usually immediately followed by having my everything on the floor. One thing that can be said for my ability to fall: I haven't missed the ground once.

I think Diane should really be a lot more careful about what she might consider getting for me in a trade. For one thing, I would imagine the after-trade cost of a couple of twenty-five year olds is still going to be pretty high. If she thinks I'm expensive to have around, just think what her monthly payments on my replacements would be.

Another consideration she should think about is the problem that occurs when people buy cars that are too much for them to handle. I'm sure the same problem might befall a wife who trades her husband in on a more powerful sports model or two. The little old lady from Pasadena might have been able to handle all that power under the hood, but I really wonder if Diane could handle the strain of trying to steer a couple young guys into doing things the way she wants them done. The workload trying to get them both to put their dirty laundry into the basket would seem to be reason enough to keep just one of me instead. After all, I still manage to hit the basket, and sometimes the clothes even land inside it.

I may not have the sleek lines of a sports car anymore, but, hey, I do carry a lot of excess baggage.

IF I HAD AN AFFAIR, SHOULDN'T I REMEMBER IT?

I read a report recently that said sex in the workplace is increasing. This doesn't do me much good, because I work alone in my home office. The best it gets around here is when one of the cats starts rubbing against my leg.

I am, however, not unfamiliar with the problems that can arise when you get involved in an affair at work. Twenty years ago I had an illicit office affair. Unfortunately, neither I, nor the person I was having it with, knew it was happening. This, of course, really takes the fun out of it.

Affairs like that are more common than you might imagine. All of the romping about occurs in the minds of people who are jumping to premature confusions. The key players miss all the fun. Everyone around the office knows they are having it. It's the talk of the office, but only when the "affairer" and the "affairee" are away "affairing", or at least out of earshot.

Often, one person is on top of the other. (I am, of course, referring to their relative location on the organization chart.) So it was between myself and a woman I'll call Angela. (I'll use that name to protect the innocent, and because her name is Angela.) At the time, she was my boss, and, as rumor had it, we had one heck of a steamy affair going on for a couple of years. I can only imagine how steamy it might have been, because it was only in the imaginations of the people we worked with.

I don't doubt for a moment that people could see we enjoyed each other's company. In their defense, all the signs that we were having an affair might have been there. We spent long hours together in the office. We'd slip away for private lunches in French restaurants. My car would be parked outside her apartment building in the morning and we'd both arrive at work together.

Any fool could see we were having an affair. One fool, in particular, took it upon himself to call my wife to let her know. I guess I should have thanked the guy. Had he not made that call, Angela and I might never have known that we were having so much fun.

Sure, we spent long hours together in the office. We were working on a special project that required a lot of work. Perhaps, since this was a government office, the sight of people actually working is what confused the others.

It's true we did slip away for private lunches in French restaurants. There wasn't anyone else in the office we'd want to eat with and, since we were working in Quebec, even the Chinese food places were French.

My car used to be parked outside her apartment building in the morning because I picked her up on the way to work and she was, and probably still is, the kind of person who will be late for her own funeral.

Thankfully, my wife knew the truth, and laughed at the informant. It would have been really upsetting to be hauled into divorce court for having an affair without ever having known about it.

WITH NOISES LIKE THAT DO WE REALLY NEED AN ALARM?

Thanks to a heightened awareness of the increasing crime rate plus a healthy dose of paranoia we decided to have a monitored alarm system installed in our new home. Our old security system wasn't that great. It combined a couple of deadbolt locks on the doors with the dumbest dog to ever get lost on a single flight of stairs. The deadbolts might have deterred the criminal element from attempting to get into the house, but I'm not convinced our cognitively challenged dog had the mentality needed to serve and protect. The only trait she shared with a well-trained police dog is an overwhelming urge to eat donuts.

We did a bit of research before calling in a security company. It seems that just about everybody has gotten into the business lately. After ruling out the company that sold alarms, cellular phones, satellite TV systems, and did contract garbage collection, we settled on a national company.

I assumed that buying a security system would be a fairly simple procedure.

It's not.

Apparently, before having a burglar alarm installed, you are required to spend a minimum of two hours in the company of the salesperson who can't deviate from the preprogrammed spiel. The first half hour is spent in the 'getting to know your customer' phase.

We didn't want a new friend. We just wanted an alarm system.

When he found out that I write newspaper columns, he became emotional and told us that he hadn't always been an alarm salesman. He used to be in the circulation department of a daily newspaper until they laid him off a few years ago. I think that might mean he had been a paperboy. It took him a while to compose himself after the emotional upset of recalling his lost job in the news media.

Eventually he pulled out his presentation kit. For the next half hour we sat through a canned presentation about the company, its history, the size of its building in Texas, and its mission statement. I haven't been that bored since I used to count knotholes in the boards behind the altar in the church I went to as a ten-year-old.

Finally, when we thought we might have to ask him to stay the night before he would get around to selling us the alarm, he asked us if we had any questions up to that point. Both Diane and I jumped at the chance to say, "Yes. How much is it going to cost?"

The answer to that question took another forty-five minutes. Apparently security system salespeople don't answer that question without first explaining every conceivable aspect of the company's operation at least three times.

Purchasing the system was just the start of the time commitment required. Five days after we had finally managed to usher the salesman out of the apartment, we met the installer. Our apartment was pre-wired for a security system. We have one door leading to the hallway, two doors to the deck, and three sliding windows — a total of six connections for the system. The installer arrived at 8:00 in the morning. He didn't finish until after 3:00 PM.

A couple of days after the alarm was installed, we made a discovery that the salesman hadn't mentioned. It fills the house with an incredible amount of noise when it goes off. Diane decided to open the living room window first thing in the morning, forgetting that she had decided to try setting the alarm before we went to bed.

The sound of "Whoooo-up! Whoooo-up! Whoooo-up!" was probably heard throughout the building and by all the ships at sea. That's to say nothing of the noise the alarm was making. I didn't realize it before, but "Whoooo-up" is the sound a wife makes when she is nearly startled into vaulting through an apartment living room window. She continued to make it until she managed to get the alarm shut off.

Aside from the window and door sensors, the alarm came with an interior motion detector. It was set up in such a way that small animals like our cats and the dumbest dog to ever bark at its mistress screaming "Whooo-up!" wouldn't accidentally trigger it. Last night, someone (Okay, it was me) set the alarm without disengaging the motion detector. I guess my wife sleepily wandering to the shower is a bit bigger than the cats or the dog. For some reason she didn't appreciate having another opportunity to have her heart kick-started into warp speed first thing in the morning by the sound the alarm makes.

You'd think she'd be happy. At least we know the system works. We also know that the dog won't sleep through a break-in.

The cats are another story.

I've gone back and checked those marriage vows again.

"Love . . . " no problem.

"Honor . . . " no problem.

Okay, I'm right. There was nothing in the vows that said anything about sharing office space.

For the past ten years, I've been working from home. It's my twelve-step program for work. I wake up, take twelve steps, and I'm at work. I don't have to deal with traffic problems (especially now that the boys have grown up and aren't fighting over early morning access to the bigger bathroom.) More importantly, I don't have to worry about getting rear-ended in the commute, although there have been a couple of near misses at major intersections like the one leading into the kitchen when everyone is in a rush for their coffee.

During the day, home has been my private realm — peaceful; quiet; and sole access to the telephone, kitchen, and stereo.

Not anymore.

A few months ago my wife changed jobs. When she was considering taking the new job she said that for the first few weeks she'd be working at home. That didn't seem to be too much of a problem. I should have known better. The definition of the word few can be vastly different between the person who is saying it and the one who is hearing it.

I thought I heard, "I'll probably be working here for eight or ten weeks."

Diane meant, "I'll be working at home until some unspecified point in the future. Won't that be special?"

You might think that a couple who has survived being married for so many years would enjoy the extra time together. I'm beginning to think that we've survived because we worked in different locations. I find myself talking to an imaginary judge and jury more often these days saying things like, "Yes, Your Honor, that's when I pulled the trigger."

My work area is at the opposite end of our apartment from hers. One might think that is enough room to keep us out of each other's hair. Who knew that the woman I've been married to for so long talks to her computer? More often than not she's telling it that it is really annoying her. All I can hear is that something has ticked her off, and being the husband around here, the only logical conclusion I can draw is that the something is probably me. It tends to break my concentration into teensy-weensy little pieces when I start thinking about all the things that I might have done to annoy her.

Okay. I admit it. That is a fairly long list.

Her work area is in what used to be our kitchen nook. This produces its own unique little annoyances. For example, if I leave dirty dishes all over the counter, or when I don't bother wiping the counter after slicing a tomato, I'm messing up "her office." Oh for the old days when I was just messing up the kitchen. Back then, if I was fast enough, I could deal with the dishes and the tomato residue before she got home from work and she'd be none the wiser. I might even start having to be tidy for crying out loud. That's just not a natural thing for a guy. I can see it now. It won't be long before she has me putting the newspaper into the newspaper rack after I'm finished with it.

Having Diane around the apartment all of the time gives her many more opportunities to think of things that I could do to make the apartment nicer. Now she even sees the dust on things that she used to be too tired to notice when she'd get home from a long day at the office. Of course, due to a deficiency in leg length, she can't reach those dusty places. I can't count the number of times she's pointed out housecleaning opportunities when I've been in the middle of something important, like watching the news updates on the sports network. Amazingly she doesn't seem to understand that, just because I'm sitting in a recliner with my eyes closed and my jaw slack, I could be contemplating an important issue for my own business.

Okay, I could be asleep too, but just the same . . .

Of course she does have one very big ace up her sleeve, when it comes to prioritizing our two businesses and determining who should be able to tie up all four of our telephone lines at once.

She makes a lot more money than I do.

Over the years my wife and I have shared quite a bit. I would, however, have been just as happy if she hadn't bothered sharing this particular strain of the flu with me.

I don't think it is the chicken flu that has everyone in Hong Kong in a flap. It might be the turkey flu because we have been eating turkey and turkey leftovers ever since Christmas. I think there are still a few packages of white meat tucked away in the freezer. That will teach me to buy a twenty-eight-pound bird.

I think Diane brought this cold/flu home from the office. I have just about narrowed down the list of her co-workers to the one responsible for passing it on to her. I've considered going into her office and strangling the life out of the guilty party, but I barely have the strength to lift my head off the pillow, let alone smother someone else with it.

My head feels like someone has been using it for a basketball. Perhaps in my sleep someone actually did, because my sinuses are still dribbling. It hurts my throat to swallow.

When I was a kid my mother would bring me a bowl of ice cream to soothe a sore throat. There is no way anyone around here would treat my like that. Even if there were ice cream in the house, my sons would eat it before any of it could be used for medicinal purposes.

When Diane was in the middle of her bout with this germ, friends gave her a glass full of brandy to take the edge off the lousy feeling. Because of other medication that I have to take every day, I am not supposed to drink anything alcoholic, so I can't even take a wee sip of the pure and pretend it's a cure.

I can't even fall back on our wedding vows in my quest for sympathy. Other husbands could point to the part that says a couple is supposed to love one another "in sickness and in health." I lost that one on a technicality. On our wedding day, my nervous young bride stumbled on the words and ended up promising to love me "in thickness and in health." The priest should have stopped the ceremony and made her say it correctly, but he just let it slide on by. As a result she has stuck by me through weight gains, but she has a church granted escape clause when I get the flu — even if she is the one who gave it to me in the first place.

Six weeks after we were married Diane had her first experience with an ailing husband. I was a student teacher in a sixth grade class, and one of the little darlings I was teaching gave me the chicken pox. I swore if I could have ever identified the culprit he or she would still be in the sixth grade today.

When you're an adult male, chicken pox have a tendency to locate themselves in a certain, rather tender part of the anatomy. It didn't take a whole lot of imagination to assume that I had contracted some unseemly social disease — not the sort of thing that a newlywed could easily explain, especially one who felt as awful as I did at that point. I remember saying repeatedly that I had no idea where those bright red spots came from or how I happened to get them. Luckily, a doctor actually made a house call to deliver the correct diagnosis. Diane was very sympathetic. She actually left the room before she started laughing.

So here I lay, aching, sneezing, sniffling, and generally feeling sorry for myself. Diane has gone back to work. The boys have returned to school. Even my dog has deserted me, preferring to sleep her day away where her master moaning and groaning about how unfair it is that he has gotten the flu doesn't awaken her every few minutes.

I guess the only way I'm ever going to find sympathy around here is if I turn to page 479 of the dictionary.

My wife doesn't want to go to my funeral.

Before people start sending her notes of congratulations for finally getting rid of me, I should point out that I am not planning to leave this mortal toil anytime soon. I hope I still have a couple score and ten to go.

I realize that this is a bit of a morbid topic, but it's been on my mind lately. In the past two months I've lost two friends to cancer. One was fifty-two and the other was sixty-nine. Both were much too young to go. I know that both Rick and Jeri would much rather be remembered with laughter than tears.

Perhaps you might think that my wife is just showing her desire to keep me around when I say she doesn't want to attend my funeral, but that has nothing to do with her recent proclamation. She just doesn't want to be there if my wishes for the way it should be presented get followed.

Diane thinks I should be satisfied with a simple, respectable service to be held sometime after she has had my remains reduced to a little box of ashes. Now I ask you, especially those of you who have been reading my column for several years, does that sound like the sort of funeral I would want?

Of course not.

Whenever I read reviews of my writing, they tend to include words like, 'irreverent', 'sardonic', and, 'Dad, you are so weird.' Since I've spent the better part of my life living up to those standards, I think it is only to be expected that my funeral should follow the theme.

If it does, Diane says she won't be there.

Apparently, the thing she really objects to is my desire to have a motion detector hidden in my coffin and attached to a tape recorder with my voice greeting the people who come up to look into the coffin. There are lots of things I could say to the people to lighten up the moment:

"Hi there. How ya doin'?"

"Hey! You made it. Thanks for coming."

"How are you? Probably better than me, eh?"

"This list they have here says you're going to drop in next Wednesday."

"Boy is it hot here, but at least it's a dry heat."

"Would you mind scratching my nose?"

"Wanna see the scar where they harvested my organs?"

With a little work, I could even have special greetings for certain people:

To editors: "Sorry, I seem to be having trouble filing this week's column from here. Why don't you come and pick it up?"

To certain relatives who know who they are: "So this is what I had to do to get you to come for a visit."

To certain other relatives who probably wouldn't recognize themselves: "No, you can't take home all the donuts."

To doctors: "Is this what you meant by 'learn to live with it?'"

To my wife: "Okay, so how are you going to get the roasting pan down from the top shelf now?"

I think doing something like this would definitely put the "f-u-n" in funerals. People who don't have any memories of my arrival would certainly never forget my departure. I really don't want people standing around with sad faces and bemoaning the fact that I'm gone. I'd much rather be remembered with laughter and surprised reactions, just like I've given everyone while I've been alive. What could be an easier way to give them a little of both than having my disembodied voice emanating from my 'disemvoiced' body?

Diane would much rather see me have a dignified memorial service. Okay, so what isn't dignified about sharing a few final words with those I leave behind? She'd have me cremated before my body even had a chance to be put on display. She thinks that would quash the idea of including a motion detector and tape recordings of my voice. Perhaps we could modify one of those fake taxidermy fish that start singing "Take Me To The River" whenever anyone walks past. My urn could have me saying things like:

"Hey! It's dark in here."

"Whew! That was some heat wave, wasn't it?"

"I guess I finally made a real ash of myself this time, didn't I?"

"See; I told you most of my weight was just water retention."

I'm not sure why Diane is so opposed to this idea. Perhaps she figures that by the time it comes around she will have heard enough from me to last her the rest of her lifetime.

I'll show her. If she doesn't let me have a little fun at my funeral I just won't speak to her again.

Husbands who let themselves get talked into sharing the clothes buying experience with their wives should probably qualify for reduced rates at psychiatrists' offices. Just agreeing to go, let alone participating in the event, is grounds for committal in several states and provinces.

Women's wear stores are hostile territory for most men. The last thing we want is to have one of our buddies walk by in the mall and see us standing beside the girdle display.

We never, ever want to give one of the guys the opportunity to say, "Hey . . . Saw you last night when you were shopping at the Tres Chic Boutique down at the Galleria. I thought you might look good in that outfit on the mannequin you were standing beside. Pink is just the right colour for you . . . "

Naturally it's embarrassing to have your friends see you in the women's wear stores, but even worse when they have no sense of style and colour. I've always thought I looked better in blue.

The real problem comes from the person who brings us there in the first place. It's the questions that we are expected to answer that give us the most grief:

"Does this pattern make me look fat?"

How are we supposed to answer that without bruises appearing on our upper arms?

"Oh, no dear, you look a lot fatter in some of your other outfits."

"Yes, dear, it makes your butt look like a roadside warning sign."

Either way, I guarantee some bruising will be involved.

"Do you think I look too old to wear this style?"

Now there's another impossible question for you. These are even harder than when I tried to understand physics in high school. If I say she looks too old to wear something that you might see barely covering Ally McBeal, then my name will be mud for insinuating that her spring chicken days are behind her. If I say she doesn't look too old in a garment that looks like something her mother might wear, she'll probably want to grind my face in the mud for not suggesting she look for a younger style.

One thing I learned the hard way a few years ago was not to say the first thing that comes to mind when my wife emerges from a changing room. It's really not a good idea to point out that you remember an aunt who had a set of drapes in that pattern.

At least the store we were in recently had a chair for the poor shmucks who get dragged in there with their wives. It was even out of clear sight of the mall corridors so I didn't have to worry about being seen. Some stores don't offer that little convenience. This one even had juice and cookies. It took me a while but I finally realized what they were doing. If they could make me comfortable and ply me with chocolate chips, I might just be lulled into a false sense of financial security.

"Sure, dear, try on another outfit, I'll just sit here by the cookies and wait for you . . . Oh yeah, that looks great . . . Buy the white one and the blue one . . . Did you see the yellow one over there . . . ? Another cookie? Yes I do believe I will . . . "

Chocolate chips have that effect on me.

When men buy clothes, they like to go in, get it over with, and get out of the store as quickly as humanly possible. Women seem to look at clothes shopping as an endurance event. I recently bought three shirts, a pair of pants, and a bathing suit in less time than Diane spent contemplating the various advantages of a blue blouse over a brown one. Still, she had to turn to me and ask if I thought the blue one made her look fat. That was just the first of many options she considered in what seemed like the eternity I spent hiding in the chair by the cookies.

To make matters worse, we have to put up with the running, anti-male commentary from the sales staff. Throughout the ordeal, I had to listen to the staff put down my gender, our lack of colour coordinating capabilities, and our general misunderstanding of the fashion industry's designs for the remaining balance on our credit cards. I might have put up an argument but that would probably just serve to limit my access to the chocolate chip cookies and juice.

"No, Dear, that one doesn't make you look too old. The little wrinkles by your eyes are what make you look old . . . "

For a number of years in the late Seventies and early Eighties, I worked for the Canadian General Standards Board, an organization housed within the Government of Canada's bureaucracy. We produced the manufacturing and installation standards for everything from breakfast cereal to home insulation. After trying a few of those high fiber cereals, I've wondered if someone got the two standards mixed up.

Standards are produced through a process of consensus between industry, consumers, and governments. The inability of anyone to reach a consensus is probably the major reason why no one ever tried to standardize housekeeping practices. The result of this standards void is that most husbands and wives disagree about the definition of adequate housekeeping.

As with most voids, there is a vacuum involved. Ours is an upright. Frankly, it really sucks. It sucks so much that it's been known to lift loose change from beneath sofa cushions. It has little lights that indicate when a section of carpet needs more passes with the business end of the unit and when the vacuum operator can move on to another patch of carpeting. This deep cleaning action leads to a housekeeping standards argument around here. Diane seems to think that its powers should be called upon with some degree of regularity. I, on the other hand, don't want to abuse this power, and believe that it should only be let out of the broom closet when it's really needed.

My definition of when a vacuuming is needed tends to be event related. If company is coming, if the dog just dragged in half a yard of topsoil, or if the cat finally cleared the hairball she has been working on for the last couple of months, then by all means it's time a vacuuming might be in order. Diane on the other hand only needs to know that the vacuum has been safely stowed away for a couple of days before she gets the ridiculous idea that the carpets might need a good going over. She seems to believe that just because you can't see dirt that doesn't mean it isn't there. I thought that theory only worked for baby pigeons and a variety of religious deities.

Trying to develop a standard for dusting would be another exercise in consensus gathering futility. I am obviously a much more accepting person than my wife. I can accept that dust invades our home. I know that if I wipe the dust off a shelf it will just call in reinforcements within a day or two to replace whatever I remove. Diane treats dust the same way she does vacuuming. She thinks I should wipe the shelves even before the dust gets thick enough to sign my name or draw a picture in. What's the point in having dust if you can't use it as an artistic medium?

Diane has another dust-related problem. She can't reach a lot of the places that dust collects around here. She can't even see it. There is no way she could know if the top of the refrigerator is dusty, but she seems to sense it. When she senses dusty buildup I am expected to do something about it. Signing my name or drawing a picture isn't what she has in mind.

I don't want people to think that dust doesn't bother me at all. There is one place in our home where dust collects faster than in any other, and this deeply concerns me. If too much dust accumulates on our TV screen I could have difficulty watching sports while my wife redoes the vacuuming and dusting in the rest of the apartment.

Men and women might have problems coming to consensus about housekeeping issues. Aside from vacuuming and dusting, disagreements about the frequency of a wide variety of chores are likely to arise in just about every household. Everything from laundry, to dishwashing, to lawn mowing could be fertile ground for a lack of consensus between partners. I've even known couples that couldn't reach an agreement about who should be responsible for the chore of refilling the ice-cube tray. Let's not even get into a discussion about how the toilet should be cleaned or whether consensus can be reached about the proper way to leave the seat.

Women, on the other hand, don't seem to have too much trouble reaching housekeeping consensus amongst themselves. There is one thing that most women are sure to agree on when it comes to household chores:

Men are slobs.

A friend of mine has been having trouble with her septic tank lately. Believe me, if you've never experienced septic tank trouble, consider yourself fortunate. She has been complaining about this problem for the last four months. I have to give her credit for lasting that long because I didn't.

The first house that Diane and I owned had a septic tank. After a few years, it started to cause us grief, and believe me 'grief' is a very mild word for the kind of trouble a septic tank can give you. We came to the conclusion that there was only one sure way to deal with the problem. Our solution worked marvelously. That tank never gave us trouble again.

We sold the house.

I've admitted before that I am not what you might consider handy around the house. My favorite power tool is the telephone, which I use to call people who are handy and who know how to use other, more functional power tools. I'm not even very good with the tools that don't need to be plugged into the wall socket. I have several scars that bear witness to old, self-inflicted wounds that have occurred when I've tried to do something 'handy'.

When you consider the fact that a screwdriver could be construed a suicidal weapon in my hands, the thought of trying to deal with a malfunctioning septic tank was about as far from my comfort zone as you could get.

Our old septic tank had taken a lot of abuse over the years. Not all of it came from inside the house. We bought the place in the summer. It was a small hobby farm about three-quarters of a mile from a river. The following spring, when the snow started to melt, we discovered that the house was only a few yards away from that river. The ground was completely saturated; to the point that we had to keep pumps running twenty-four hours a day just to keep the water level in the basement manageable. By manageable, I mean that we could have managed to stock the basement with trout, or we might have managed to use it for an indoor pool.

I wasn't alone. My neighbor was burning out almost as many pumps as I was keeping the water below hip wader depth in his basement.

"Gord," he said, "we're just not getting the water far enough away from our foundations. We pump it out and it just flows right back in again."

We went through several bottles of my beer trying to solve our common problem. It always seemed that common problems needed my beer to inspire a solution. He never seemed to have any of his own when a problem arose. Suddenly, he jumped up and did what most people do after drinking several bottles of their neighbor's beer. He staggered to the john.

Like so many other brilliant ideas through history, his trip down the hall led him face to face with the solution to our flooded basements. "If we connect our pumps to the septic tank, we could pump the water out through the tile bed, and away from our basements,' he slurred, upon returning from his call from Nature.

It was such an obvious solution, neither of us could understand why some of the farmers who had lived in the area for decades hadn't thought of it before.

Since it was his idea, it was only fair that we worked on his house first. My neighbor was one of those people you might call 'handy'. It didn't take him long to fashion a device to connect the pump to the pipe that led through his basement wall to the septic tank out back.

We were really quite pleased that our wives weren't around. Solving the flooded basement problem would be a great surprise. They'd be really impressed with our ingenuity.

They were surprised all right, but not nearly as surprised as we were when we tried to undo the thread on the valve that led to the septic tank. Apparently, the high water table that was feeding so much water into our basements was also preventing the septic tank from draining properly. Before he finished unscrewing the cap at the bend in the pipe just before it passed through the wall, the pressure stripped the remaining threads and the contents of the septic tank flew through the opening, hitting my neighbor squarely in the chest. It drove him backwards, across his basement.

He only had time to say one word. I'm not sure if he was using the term as a curse, or if he was describing the stuff hitting him in the chest. The same word could be used quite effectively either way.

It was a moment that made me glad I'm not 'handy'. It was also a moment that made me glad we worked on his house first. I can only imagine my wife's reaction to several hundred gallons of sewage spread across the basement floor.

And it scares 'that word my neighbor used' out of me to even think about it.

I guess I finally have to admit that winter is just around the corner. Okay, maybe it's not right around the corner, but it's definitely around the corner and up the mountain a couple of thousand feet.

When the clouds cleared away this morning there was snow on the mountain outside my office window — lots of it. Thankfully, it's still about 3000 feet up, but that's still about 3000 feet too close for my comfort.

It's not that I don't like snow. I thoroughly enjoy seeing scenes of snowy landscapes elsewhere in the country. I just don't like to see the stuff in my driveway. Knowing that there is a snow-capped peak just behind my left shoulder as I work at my computer gives me the feeling that someone is watching me. I'm not normally a paranoid person, but I firmly believe that the snow is waiting for its chance to sneak down the mountain and catch me unaware.

Winter brings a lot of personal safely issues to mind. Because I have to use crutches to walk, snow and ice present me with more than the usual hazards. I'm not afraid to drive in a blizzard, but a dusting of snow between the front door and the car door can scare the heck out of me. I need someone to invent steel belted radial snow tires for the bottom of my crutches.

I never had any idea that cold weather could also present a danger to me inside the house. My wife, whose body temperature can fluctuate from "I'm absolutely frozen," to "Is it just me or is it really hot in here," in a matter of seconds, tried to kill me with the fireplace.

Diane avoids gas appliances with a complete determination. She witnessed a gas explosion that leveled a few houses, and killed the backhoe operator who dug through a gas line, just a couple of weeks before we were married. She is convinced that lighting the gas barbecue might do the same thing to her. She has passed that fear on to the dog. Nipper just has to see me with a box of matches in my hand and she will run for cover making noises like she thinks the world is coming to an end.

Having lived with her fear for the last twenty-five years, I should have been suspicious when she tried to light the gas fireplace in the living room. It's easy to light. You just turn a little knob, and the pilot light does the rest. Somehow, Diane managed to extinguish the pilot light.

Even after the events that transpired over the next couple of minutes, she still claims she didn't do it on purpose.

When I suggested she re-light the pilot light, she gave me one of her patented, deer-in-the-headlights looks that wordlessly told me what I could do with that idea.

It took me a couple of minutes to find the box of matches. The first threat to my life and limbs came when I nearly tripped over the dog as she ran for cover when she saw what I had in my hand.

After striking the match and approaching the pilot light with it I realized instantly that something was amiss. Normally, it takes about thirty seconds for the pilot light to re-ignite. Not this time. In her haste to get away from the fireplace, Diane hadn't turned off the gas.

Bright blue flames jumped from the pilot light before the match was anywhere near it. Flames sprang from the entire fireplace a split millisecond later.

I didn't spring. I sat frozen to the spot. I could not move, but I was afraid that my bowels just might. The room was quiet, except for the sound of the dog falling down the stairs in her haste to escape. Diane didn't say a word. I couldn't say a word. I just sat there staring at the fireplace, still holding the match in my hand. Thankfully, the rush of air that followed the fire up the chimney sucked the flame right off the match, thereby preventing further injury.

I did a quick personal inventory. I was relieved to discover that I was still in possession of all my fingers, my hair, and my beard.

Diane, of course, denied any responsibility. She claimed that if she had intentionally tried to blow me up with the fireplace, she wouldn't have sat on the couch to watch. I'd like to believe her. After so many years of marriage, you don't want to start worrying about your wife sabotaging gas appliances.

. . . if only she'd stop laughing about it.

My wife has a new hole in her head.

No, I didn't put it there. She had a tooth pulled last week. Life, as we know it around here, has not been the same since.

Like most husbands, I have learned how to deal with my wife when she is upset about something. (I hide.) I've even learned how to cope with it when she's angry. (I hide better.) Pain, though, is another story. Few husbands can deal with their wives in pain. We don't know what to do. If we don't behave compassionately enough we have to come up with an entirely new self-preservation method. (We can run, but we cannot hide.)

There isn't a husband alive who has been at his wife's side in the delivery room who wouldn't sympathize with my plight. Women in pain have a powerful effect on the men in their lives.

They scare the bejeepers out of us.

The biggest fear that men face when confronted by an aching spouse is that she will somehow find a way to blame us for her situation. I'm sure one of the most common phrases heard in delivery rooms throughout North America is, "You did this to me!"

Our male paranoia kicks in when our wives have headaches. ("I don't know how she got the headache, but it's most likely my fault.") Even when there is absolutely no way that the pain she is feeling can be linked — directly or indirectly — back to us, we are still afraid that the blame is somehow going to come home to roost on our shoulders.

I hoped the Novocain injected into her gums would buy me some time to think up all the reasons why the pain she would be feeling was the dentist's fault, not mine. Unfortunately, I forgot the level of importance wives put on marital communications. All husbands know, however, that even when a communication problem occurs with our spouses that is not even remotely our fault, it is still completely and unequivocally our fault. Let's face it, if a communications breakdown occurs, nine times out of ten it's going to be our fault anyway. A wise husband knows in that remaining one time out of ten, he should take responsibility, just for the sake of continuity.

When Diane returned from the dentist's office last week she gave me explicit instructions about what she wanted me to do. Unfortunately, I could not understand a word she was saying. The dentist had used a great deal of freezing in her jaw, and it severely reduced her communications capabilities.

"I beeb boo boo bo boo ba bore," she said.

"Uhh . . . Okay, Dear," I replied, hoping that sooner or later, I could figure out what she was trying to tell me.

Eventually, through sheer luck, I determined that she needed me to go to the store. Unfortunately, that was the last thing I understood.

"Be beeb bilk, bab bi beeb boo boo bick ub by babicbun," she explained.

I knew I was in serious trouble. My wife was talking like a Teletubby.

Since I had already determined that I was supposed to go to the store, I thought it might win me a bit of a reprieve if I just nodded sympathetically, and told her I wouldn't be gone too long. That seemed to satisfy her, but I knew that I wouldn't stand a chance if I didn't come back with whatever it was she was saying I should get.

I did the only sensible thing I could think of. I hope wives everywhere marvel at this. To think that a husband actually thought of a solution all by himself seems beyond the realm of believability. In fact, I'm pretty proud of myself to have thought this out so clearly, when I was obviously under a lot of pressure to get the job done.

So what was this fantastic solution? I went to the dentist's office, knowing that since they are forever making people talk that way, someone there could probably translate for me.

"Oh, that's easy," said the receptionist, "You need milk and she wants you to pick up her prescription."

I wanted to bring the woman home to act as a translator until the freezing wore off.

My father had it much easier. A child's strength painkiller could knock out my mother for several hours. Whenever she went to the dentist, it was usually several days before she was conscious enough to talk, and by then the freezing would have all worn off so she could be understood.

On one occasion, my father was delayed getting to the dentist's office by a horrific snowstorm. By the time he arrived the painkillers had already kicked in. He and the dentist had to carry my mother to the car, where she sat, slumped against the window, completely unaware of my father's presence, the snowstorm, the pain in her mouth, or her own appearance.

The drive home was a long and difficult journey because of the snow. Eventually, my father had to stop for gas. The attendant looked in the open window and saw my mother, out cold, with her head against the far window, and a small trickle of blood on her chin.

No doubt he was convinced that my father had heard all he wanted to about how he was driving in the snowstorm, how long it was taking to get home, and that he had reached across the front seat of the car and popped my mother a good one in the jaw, knocking her out.

I should be so lucky. It's now been five days since Diane's tooth was pulled. I'm still hearing about how much her mouth hurts. I try to be sympathetic, compassionate, and all those other things that the relationship books say we should be doing in situations like this. It's clear, however, that whoever wrote those books never had to deal with a wife in pain.

Hunters know that a wounded animal can be extremely dangerous. Next time something like this happens, I'm going to get a tranquilizer gun. I'll shoot myself with it to put me out of her misery — at least until the pain goes away.

Like most men, I have to admit there is an awful lot I don't fully understand about women. Maybe it has something to do with chromosomes. Whatever it is, something causes normally intelligent men to sit and scratch their heads in wonder at the actions of the opposite sex. We just don't get it most of the time.

I don't understand why I have to fight through a jungle of pantyhose legs to get to the shower. I don't understand why going to the store requires twenty minutes of preparation time with a curling iron. It's beyond me why money left in a shirt pocket overnight is no longer my money. I can't explain how a woman can enjoy watching a show like *The X-Files*, where someone is regularly getting disemboweled by supernatural forces, and still think hockey is too violent.

I don't care how smart a man might be, we just aren't meant to understand these things. One thing that absolutely defies the cognitive capabilities of men everywhere is a woman's purse. Einstein might have been able to figure out that $e=mc^2$ thing, but there is absolutely no way he could have ever come close to determining the forces of nature that come into play inside a woman's purse.

My wife bought a new purse the other day. I had the unfortunate bit of bad luck to be trapped in the car beside her while she transferred everything that had been in her old purse to the new one.

Men have wallets and pockets that carry everything they need — on rare occasions we might be able to find a bit of money in one or the other. Purses, on the other hand, carry a myriad of stuff that makes little or no sense to me.

Looking at her purse brings up a lot of questions:

Why does she need to have five pens in her purse? Is she planning on becoming ambidextrous and developing the ability to write with her feet and mouth too?

Why does she need a purse with a cell phone pocket when she doesn't turn her cell phone on, just in case someone might call her and use up some of the time she pays for each month?

Does she really need more keys than a school janitor or a jail guard?

Has she thrown out a sales receipt since we were married in 1973?

Just thinking about answering questions like that makes my brain hurt.

I want to point out that my wife is a very smart woman. She has a much stronger grip on math and sciences than I ever could hope to develop. That's why it seems so strange that she cannot see the correlation between the size of the purse she bought and the cubic mass of the stuff she wants to carry around with her. Some women buy shoes a size too small to make their feet look smaller. My wife buys a purse a size or two too small to make it look like she isn't carrying around a medicine cabinet, a make-up kit, her own personal version of the Smithsonian Institute, and more paper than it takes to produce a copy of the *Encyclopedia Britannica*.

By the time she loaded the new purse, Mike Tyson couldn't have gotten that thing closed. He just doesn't have that much strength in his arms. After transferring a checkbook, a prescription bottle, and several hundred thousand pieces of paper into my glove box and the map pockets on the door, she finally managed to get the snap to close. The purse sat there quivering on her lap looking like it was ready to blow. If it went off, I knew we would both die.

I can picture the police investigating that explosion saying, "There's only one thing known to man that could possibly have caused that much destruction. Forget TNT, nitroglycerine, or plastique. This kind of damage could only have been inflicted by an overstuffed woman's purse. We may have to evacuate the area because of the possibility of aftershocks."

I've told Diane that I really don't want her to keep that purse in the bedroom at night. The vibrations from the dog falling off the end of our bed could set the thing off and blow us all into oblivion.

Perhaps men aren't supposed to understand things like purses, the drying process for pantyhose, and how long it takes a woman to curl her hair before being seen in public. I'm fine with that . . .

. . . just as long as I never have to go near that purse without protective clothing.

I'm going to kill my wife.

Now, before all of the anti-violence against women advocates get up in arms and call for my immediate crucifixion, I'd like to point out that she is going to kill me, too. Fair is fair. If I'm going to get killed I should get to do a little killing myself.

No, I'm not talking about some bizarre murder-suicide plot that we are hatching in our kitchen because of a bad case of empty-nest syndrome induced depression. A headline on this morning's paper made it all quite clear. She's killing me and I'm killing her. It said, "Loving your spouse can drive you to an early grave."

The article opened with the following statement: "If your husband is the strong silent type he might be helping both of you live longer." Anyone who knows me will tell you that I don't quite fit into the mold of the strong and silent type. At my size I don't fit too well into any mold.

The article went on to say, " . . . if you share a close supporting relationship, then you could be driving each other to an early death. The secret to living longer together is to have a strong, independent husband with the wife leaning on him emotionally, according to a six year study."

Diane and I have been married for over thirty years. I think we're both pretty supportive of each other. All along I thought it was the way a good marriage was supposed to be. Now I find out that that all this love stuff is killing us. I could have maintained my independence on the grounds that I was helping her live longer. Mind you, if I had she probably would have gotten rid of me a long time ago.

Frankly, if Diane tried to lean on me without offering me an equal amount of support, we'd probably both fall flat on my support mechanism. That's either going to be my wheelchair or my crutches, and either way, it's probably going to hurt.

It's all supported by research done by the Gerontological Society of America. They studied 305 couples to determine which ones might still be alive after a six-year period. In the closest couples, the ones who lean on each other for support, the wife was nine times more likely to die and the husband four times more likely. If the wife remained independent she became eleven times more likely to die than the husband who leaned on her who was five times more likely kick the proverbial bucket.

According to the study, Diane might be in more trouble because we had children. Even though, like ours, they may have escaped the tyranny of their parent's dictatorial regime, offspring still tend to depend on their mothers for emotional support more than they lean on the dear old dads of the world. This heavier load on the women might factor in to their earlier demise. I doubt it because, as a long-standing loving husband, I know that everything is my fault just because I am a husband.

Therefore the kids remain blameless in her rush to the grave.

There is a chance that we might not be influenced the way the study shows. The researchers' back door to get them out of making a definitive statement is that Baby-Boomers might not be as conflicted about their roles as today's older couples are. At last, there's something good about being a Boomer that I can show my Generation-X sons.

Still, on the chance that Diane is killing me with love, I need to get my affairs in order. That way she will still have something of me around to remind her of our wonderful years together. I obviously need to take a good look at my will to make certain provisions to maintain my legacy.

I think that I should have my body cremated. My ashes could then be spread around the apartment so that she could continue to spend the rest of her life picking up after me. You might think she could solve that with a good vacuuming, but I should point out that Diane is only 5' 4". She can't see many of the places that dust settles around here. Part of me could spend years up on top of the refrigerator. In a similar vein, I might leave some money to pay for someone to sneak into our home every day and leave socks and underwear on the bedroom floor.

It would be like I had never really left.

My Family Is Growing Up,
But I Refuse To

The holiday season is supposed to bring forth fond memories of Christmases past. One memory of mine that always seems to come to the forefront at this time of year doesn't fit in the "fond" category. I still shudder whenever I hear "Oh Christmas Tree" on the radio, or see a display of Christmas tree stands in a hardware store.

The economy hit us hard just before Christmas in 1985. The company I was working for had fallen on hard times. As a result, we were faced with the task of trying to cut costs wherever we could. Despite our lack of excess liquid capital, we wanted Christmas to be as normal as possible for the boys who, at the time, were just three and five.

We found a lot offering trees starting at just $3.99. The 'trees', it turned out, were branches cut from giant Douglas Firs. The trunks had gone off to become newsprint and Christmas cards, and someone had gotten the bright idea to sell the smaller branches as Christmas trees.

Christmas trees and I often have disagreements about how they are supposed to behave. Over the years I have tried all kinds of Christmas tree stands. No matter how great the stand is supposed to be, I still end up with trees that lean several degrees off vertical. Even if I decided to drill a hole in the floor, insert the tree, and pour in a foot of concrete, I would still have to tie the top of the tree to two walls to prevent it from tipping.

When I attempted to erect the tree/branch, I turned the holding bolts on the stand until they would turn no more. None of them reached wood. The tree just wobbled between the bolts. In my calm quiet manner, I hammered blocks of wood around the bottom of its trunk. Eventually, the tree cooperated and looked as though it just might make it through the season without collapsing.

The next morning I took my youngest, Brad, to his preschool Christmas pageant. The tree was still standing, which was a good sign, but I decided that it would probably be a good idea to tie it to the wall with another wire when we returned.

The children presented a Christmas song and dance routine that their teacher had written. As they sang, they all put on pretend coats and hats. They put pretend axes over their shoulders, and walked across the stage to find their "Cwithmath twee." They chopped down the imaginary tree, put their pretend ax over one shoulder and the trunk of their tree over the other, and walked back across the stage home.

They all got down on their knees and put their tree in its stand. They stood up and put the lights around it. Brad was still on his knees. They put on the ornaments. Brad was still on his knees. They put the star on top. They hung foil icicles from the bows.

Just as the rest of the children began to put pretend presents under their pretend trees, Brad, still on his knees, turned to the audience and said, in a voice that carried throughout the room and to all the ships at sea, the words that haunt me to this day.

"I can't get this freaking twee in the freaking stand!"

Unfortunately, he did not use the word 'freaking', but another that sounded somewhat similar.

I thought that perhaps if I looked around the room, pretending to look for that boy's parents, the other parents in that church basement would bypass me in their search. All I wanted from the Santa who was holding himself up with the wall in the corner Ho-Ho-Ho-ing loudly was a bit of simple anonymity.

But Noooooooooooooo!

I had his brother along, and he seemed determined to eliminate that wish. He stood on his chair and loudly asked me, "Is Brad going to get in trouble for saying that?"

"He really shouldn't have said, 'freaking tree,' should he, Dad?"

"Are you going to tell Mom that he said, 'freaking tree'?"

"Why did you call our tree 'the freaking tree' Dad?"

"Mom said you shouldn't have said, 'freaking tree'. She says it's not a word to be repeated. Brad sure repeated it didn't he Dad?"

"Daddy, why do you have your head between your knees?"

When my wife returned home that night, Mike had the story of the afternoon's events, with appropriate emphasis on the word his brother used, retold before she could get her coat off. After a few gasps, and a stifled laugh, she gave me one of those looks that told me on which one of Santa's lists I could probably find my name.

Just my freaking luck.

My son Brad set down the phone, came into my office, and asked me for fifty dollars. He told me it was for his introductory lesson. Since he had just gotten his learner's permit, I assumed he needed the money to pay for drivers' ed.

I really should have learned by now not to assume when it comes to anything my sons tell me. I should be more skeptical when it comes to their statements, even when they sound like they have a certain amount of logic behind them. Naturally, I didn't think about that when I agreed to the fifty dollars.

I heard him go back to the phone and say, "Okay, Saturday at 8:00 AM would be fine."

I was proud of him taking things into his own hands. He'd probably called the same driving school that his brother had gone to a couple of years ago. I was even mildly surprised that he was actually willing to be someplace at 8:00 AM on a Saturday, when, like most teenage boys, he normally wouldn't be conscious before at least noon on a weekend.

When he got off the phone, he came back to my office looking like a cat that had just swallowed a bird.

"I'll need a ride to my lesson, first thing Saturday morning," he said. "Can you get me there by 8:00 AM?"

I wanted to be one of those supportive parents like we see in TV sitcoms. I agreed to drive him, despite a strong willingness on my part to be still asleep when 8:00 AM rolled around on Saturday. When I asked him where he wanted me to take him I discovered that we had been speaking the same language, but not about the same things.

"The airport, of course," he said, as though I shouldn't have needed to ask.

I tried to picture where there was a driving school near the Pitt Meadows International Airport And Chinese Food Restaurant, but, like so often happens when I try to think and communicate with one of my sons at the same time, I drew a blank.

"It's got nothing to do with getting my driving license, Dad," he said. "I'm going for my introductory flying lesson."

My thought blockage suddenly cleared. My mind was suddenly flooded with questions. How did I let myself get talked into this? How am I going to explain this expenditure to my personal banker, also known as my wife? As scary as that last thought was, it paled in comparison to the next one that flew through my brain: Will I have to go in the plane with him?

My facial expression probably gave away what I was thinking, because Brad immediately assured me that it would just be him and the instructor going up for the flight. He actually had the audacity to insinuate that I might be afraid of heights or of flying.

Nothing could be further from the truth. I am not afraid of heights, nor am I afraid of flying. Falling from a great height scares the heck out of me though. Even worse, I am absolutely terrified of plane crashes. I can't think of a worse way to ruin your day than to be happily flying along, not being afraid of the fact that you are 35,000 feet above the ground, only to have your bliss interrupted by an unexpected plane crash.

Not that I would have gone back on my word, even though I do feel I was tricked into agreeing to foot the bill for the lesson, but Brad started working on all of the advantages I would enjoy if he were to get his pilot's license. He could, for example, fly me to my appearances around the country. That's assuming that I would pay for the fuel, the rental of the aircraft, and an hourly rate for his piloting. Somehow I think I could buy a lot of airline tickets for the same amount of money.

Before you start thinking that I'm not the supportive parent I make out to be, I want you to know that I have, in fact, encouraged him to go for it. It will cost about $7,000 for all of the lessons, plane rentals, and fuel to get his private pilot's license. I told him the same thing that I told his brother when he came home with the idea that he'd like to go to Europe a couple of years ago.

"I think it's a great idea. Let me know as soon as you've figured out how you are going to pay for it."

Believe me, I put a lot of emphasis on the phrase "you are going to pay for it."

I've undertaken an archeological expedition of great proportions. I don't anticipate finding a pharaoh's tomb, the lost city of Atlantis, or the treasure of Black Beard, but I am finding a few interesting artifacts.

I'm emptying our freezer.

I'm sure that we aren't unusual. We go to the store, buy groceries, put them in the freezer, and lose them when we repeat the process a couple of weeks later and bury the stuff that was already there with new stuff. Eventually, some things just naturally settle to the bottom of the freezer, not to be seen again until someone mounts an expedition like this. I set out on this one to disprove a claim by our resident teenager that there isn't any food in the house. It's a ridiculous idea. The freezer is half-full.

Like any good archeological dig, one of the things I found was a collection of bones belonging to several long deceased animals. It would appear that on at least five separate occasions, we have carefully packaged the bones from Christmas and Thanksgiving turkeys and put them in the freezer for that future day when we would all gather around the table for homemade turkey soup.

As good as home-made turkey soup might sound, no one around here ever seemed the least bit inclined to haul a turkey carcass out of the freezer and go to the effort of making the stuff. Still, each holiday meal seemed to instill some sort of uncontrolled enthusiasm for homemade turkey soup. Each carcass went into the freezer without a thought for the one, two, three, or four carcasses that had preceded it into the abyss. Eventually, the carcasses became buried by other purchases, and, just like in nature, the bones were buried deep below the surface.

Archeologists are able to learn a lot about long lost civilizations by the utensils that are found around the sites of old villages, in caves, and buried beneath the sands of time. My project yielded some startling finds of this nature. I found four stainless steel soup spoons, two butter knives, three dessert spoons, and a plastic ice cream scoop. Two of the soup spoons were found inside a plastic bucket that contained a few remnants of what looked like cookie dough ice cream. Minute bits of rainbow swirl ice cream were frozen to the plastic scoop.

The utensils in the freezer, to say the least, puzzled me. After a great deal of thought I came to what seemed to me a reasonable explanation. I think someone has been breaking into our house at night to steal pieces of our cutlery. When they are making their daring getaway, they pass the freezer. Looking inside they see that we have ice cream. Using the spoon that they have conveniently secreted away from the kitchen drawer, they start eating directly out of the ice cream bucket. That's when they must be scared off by dog, who wakes up when she smells the ice cream — or perhaps the frozen pizzas — and goes looking for a handout. The would-be robber flees the scene, leaving the utensil in the freezer.

The only other possible answer to this mystery is that one of our resident teenagers eats ice cream directly from the freezer so that he doesn't have to waste energy carrying a bowl down from the kitchen. In a similar, energy conserving move he leaves the spoon in the freezer rather than waste the energy carrying it back up the stairs to the dishwasher.

Archeologists learned a lot about early man from the remnants of food left behind in caves. I'm not sure that any of them could identify some of the leftovers that we've left behind at the bottom of the freezer in small plastic containers and freezer bags. Between the buildup of ice crystals, and the loss of structural integrity caused by years of resting in a cryogenic state, I had no idea what most of the packages contained. I don't think I will ever be hungry enough to try thawing and consuming the remains of a meal that I no longer recognize.

I even found a few items that brought back nostalgic memories. There are still a few packages of frozen smoked salmon from my last fishing trip. That was a great time. My youngest son and I both caught fish. He had just finished sixth grade. He'll graduate from high school in a few months.

I've learned something from all of this research into the deep dark history of the Kirkland family freezer. My son is right . . .

. . . there isn't any food in the house.

GETTING THERE IS STILL
A HIGH SCHOOL STUDENT'S BIGGEST CHALLENGE

To say that my youngest son is a morning person would be, among other things, an out-and-out, barefaced, shameless lie of fairly momentous proportions.

While his older brother could sleep through alarm clocks, the cannon passage of the *1812 Overture* at full blast, and a limited nuclear war, Brad does regain consciousness when his alarm goes off. He just doesn't want to accept what it means. As a result, I am often faced with one of two requests. If I am home, I'm asked to drive him the three blocks to school in an effort to assist him in avoiding garbage pick-up duty for being late. If that fails, he tells me he needs a note explaining why he failed to drag his sorry butt into the hallowed halls of Pitt Meadows Secondary, a.k.a. 'Good Old P.M.S.', on time.

Despite hating it when I hear my parents words coming from my mouth, I have tried all of the various lectures about the importance of getting into the habit of waking up at the same time every day and getting to school on time. I stress, just as my mother and father did, that someday getting to work late might have more dire consequences than garbage detail. Somehow, I am less than convincing if I am telling him this from my bed at a time when I too should already have started my day.

I've also tried out many of the exaggerated stories that my parents told in an attempt to shame me into realizing just how soft I had it when it came to getting to school on time in the morning. Most parents have used the stories about five miles of waist deep snow, uphill both ways to school and back. I don't have much credibility with the ones about feeding the chickens, milking the cows, and cleaning stalls, especially after my sons found out that I spent my high school years living on the 9th floor of an apartment building.

Despite not having chickens to feed or cows to milk, I do contend that there is a huge difference between the struggles of getting to school on time that I faced and the one that has challenged my sons. Good Old P.M.S. is three blocks from our house. Even sleepwalking, the average teenager should be able to traverse that difficult terrain in something less than three or four hours. I, on the other hand, did indeed live a full five miles from my high school. Not only was there not a school bus, the city bus company had not seen fit to run one along the street to my school, even though it was the busiest thoroughfare in the entire city. As a result, I hitchhiked.

I realize that times have changed and hitchhiking is far more dangerous today than it was in the prehistoric times that I went to school. I wouldn't encourage my sons to hitchhike to school, not because I don't think they could take care of themselves, but because there really isn't enough traffic on our suburban street to give them much of a chance to get picked up. Even if they did, it breaks several cardinal rules of hitchhiking to get into the car of someone nice enough to stop for you, and then tell them that you are only going three blocks.

When I used to stick my thumb out along the side of the road, I was always fairly lucky. I don't recall ever being late for school because of a lack of sympathetic drivers. More often than not one of my teachers would see me standing there and prevent me from missing my first class of the day by picking me up.

Not all drivers were as kind. I remember one in particular, a girl about my age, who often drove her father's car to school when he was out of town. It was a big car. It probably could have held her and four or five hitchhikers, but she seemed oblivious to that fact. In rain, sleet, snow, wind, or blazing sun, she ignored my thumb. To make matters worse, she would occasionally wave at me as she drove by in the comfort of that car. I could not understand how she could do that to me. After all, I was a nice guy, albeit a 6' 4" nice guy with shoulder length hair, a full beard, and a fringed buckskin leather jacket, but hey, it was 1969. I could never figure out why she wouldn't give me a ride.

Diane always points out that when she saw me she did more than just drive past. She locked her car doors, too.

We had a slightly poignant event occur recently. After nearly fifteen years, another parenting ritual has come to an end. As your children grow, you have these sorts of things crop up every so often — the last visit of the tooth fairy; the final little league or minor hockey game; the last diaper change . . .

Okay, so some of them aren't as bittersweet as others, but you get the point.

Since 1985, my wife and I have gone out twice a year to parent teacher interviews. That's thirty evenings spent listening to descriptions of our sons' skills, or lack thereof. We've sat down with a total of ninety-seven teachers. We've looked at ninety-seven sets of textbooks and teachers' records of our sons' aptitude at writing tests, exams, and book reports. With our youngest about to graduate from high school, we just went through it for the last time.

I wish now that I had taken the opportunity to keep a record of the things we learned about our sons by attending these events. At times we left thinking that the teacher might have confused us with some other student's parents. I've often wondered if a teacher was really talking about my son when he or she said that "he's a quiet, well mannered boy," especially when they were talking about the one who, at the age of four, silenced an entire restaurant with an extremely loud outburst, complete with a fairly graphic explicative, after spilling a glass of milk.

At times I've been confused by the marks my sons were getting in particular subjects. My high school physics teacher would probably question my involvement in their genetic heritage because both of them aced the subject that I barely managed to squeak through. On the other hand, there was no question that they had inherited their lack of prowess in French from my side of the family.

There were a couple of other unscheduled parent teacher appointments that we had to attend over the years. Both involved my youngest son.

When Brad was in grade five, my wife and I were summoned to a meeting with the teacher, the school principal, and the parish priest responsible for the school. My son had committed a great sin — one that would eventually mean the end of his days at that particular school.

He made a paper airplane.

To hear the teacher, the principal, and the priest talk you'd think the child had torn a page from the Guttenberg Bible and transformed it into a sleek, aerodynamic glider. One would almost expect that his punishment might involve tying him to a stake and building a large bonfire beneath his feet.

It turned out that the offending airplane was folded using a slip of paper that the teacher had given him to bring home to me. On it, photocopied about thirty degrees askew, was a notice that said he had not done his homework. As it was, the boy had done his homework, but left it on my desk because I was supposed to sign it indicating that I had reviewed it with him.

I forgot.

Brad's defense was that he was folding the piece of paper to put it into his pocket and, as he folded, he created the airplane. In his words, his teacher saw what he had done and "threw a hissy-fit."

I'm not sure why the parish priest had to get involved in the meeting. I have never heard of a commandment that says, "Thou shalt not engage in origami." We left that meeting with a clear understanding that our paper airplane folder was not welcome back at the school the next year.

Another unplanned parent teacher meeting resulted when the same son mistakenly chose the wrong selection offered by the spell check feature on the computer. His composition about space aliens with huge dangling tentacles took on an entirely different slant when the computer changed every use of the word "tentacles" to "testicles".

As Diane and I left the school the other night, it struck us that we had just ended another era of parenting. We mentioned it to another parent who was walking beside us. She suggested that Diane and I should go out for a drink to mark the occasion. It seemed like a good idea, until we remembered the money we had just spent on graduation pictures and a school ring. We'd soon be digging into our wallets for grad ceremony tickets, a tuxedo rental and countless other 'end of school' expenses.

We limited the celebration to a couple of bottles of cola.

I marked the occasion by folding the receipt into a paper airplane.

I'm confused.

I realize that that won't come as a surprise to most of my readers. It certainly is the conclusion that members of my family came to many years ago. Actually, it's their fault.

My oldest son came home from college for the weekend, which isn't overly confusing. He needs to come home every so often to ensure that he has clean clothes and at least an occasional meal that does not involve prepackaged macaroni and cheese. Still, he is the source of much of my confusion.

He brought one of his classmates home. They each brought computers with them that were far bigger than what I am used to using. One had a seventeen-inch monitor; the other had a nineteen-inch. I was immediately struck with a bad case of monitor envy. They turned our family room into something that looked like the Engineering Department on the Starship Enterprise. Even that wasn't overly confusing.

The thing that really confused me was the fact that after just six months of college, my son no longer speaks English. I'm not sure what language it is, but they were throwing around all kinds of words that weren't part of my vocabulary. In fact, they weren't even part of my dictionary's vocabulary. For all I knew, they were talking about me in Klingon.

Occasionally, a word or two would pop up that I recognized, but this was generally limited to words like 'the', 'I," and the universal teenage phrase "Is there anything to eat around here." The rest of the time they spoke in some sort of computerish.

It was enough to give Bill Gates a headache.

Most of what they were saying was in anagrams. DVD this, and SDRAM that. I was concerned until I found out that C+ is a programming language, not the grades they're getting. To me, Java Script sounds like a coupon for a free cup of coffee. To them it means, well, I'm not exactly sure what it means, but it has nothing to do with hot beverages.

I assumed that we could have a normal discussion over the dinner table. Unfortunately, the boys mentioned the problems they were having with their accounting course. I knew, as soon as they started that I was once again out of my realm. Accounting, and trying to understand corporate finances, sounds just a little too much like math for my liking. I'm one of those people who firmly believe that my bank account will never be overdrawn as long as I keep a supply of checks that I haven't written on yet. My wife, who is a stock broker, jumped right into that discussion. I had absolutely no idea what any of them were talking about. Pretty soon I was hearing terms like, 'no load funds', 'yield formulas', and 'bond maturation'.

I know for a fact that the word maturation would never have been spoken at the dinner table when I was growing up. My mother would have thought that it was something that could make you go blind. She would hyperventilate every time someone managed to slip the word 'groin' into the conversation. Naturally, my brother, sister, and I found innumerable opportunities to use groin in our dinner table discussions.

"Oh my, I've dropped a forkful of peas on my groin."

"Did this roast beef come from the cow's groin, Mom?"

We may have been rotten kids, but I'm sure my mother was never confused by anything we said.

The final evidence that I am totally and irrecoverably confused came during that same mealtime. Mike has always followed in my footsteps when it comes to a general dislike and distrust of anything resembling a cooked vegetable. In fact, when compared with Mike, you would think I am a vegetarian. You can imagine my complete and utter confusion when I watched him put a pile of cooked carrots onto his plate. Now it wasn't just his words that had me bewildered. He was not acting like the same son who had rebelled at green pepper in his salad because he didn't care for its texture.

I did what any concerned father would do in that situation.

I checked his forehead to see if he was running a fever.

Yesterday I was trying to make some hotel reservations on one of those 800 line reservation systems. The woman asked all the usual details, credit card number, name, and address. After she asked me for the town I live in, she said, " . . . and what state are you in?"

"Confusion," I said, "I'm most definitely in the state of confusion."

My friend Peder (yes, that's how you spell his name because, through no fault of his own, he's Danish) sent me an e-mail this morning listing all of the things that kids starting college this year are too young to remember. It was produced by the staff of Beloit College in Wisconsin to make it easier for professors to understand today's freshmen. It's great to have friends who send me stuff like that. It's usually enough to get me to phone my doctor and ask for some sample packages of Prozac. It got me thinking about the differences and similarities between when I started university in 1972 and my son's freshman beginnings this year.

The fact that it has been over thirty years since my parents dropped me off in front of a dorm is a bit disconcerting. I did the math in my head twice, and then decided that I had better confirm it with a calculator. That made me remember that the pocket calculator wasn't around when I started university. My first one cost me a hundred dollars, and could only add, subtract, multiply, and divide. When he was about three, Brad got a free one in a box of cereal that could calculate square roots, percentages, and convert the metric system into something his mother could understand.

Brad of course is doing all of his term papers on a laptop computer. That would have made life a lot easier for me back then, but it wasn't something that even crossed our minds. Oh, sure, there were computers in existence, but if someone had set one on my lap, it would have resulted in an immediate, and probably a somewhat less than sterile, amputation. We had typewriters, though. We thought we were working with the pinnacle of technology when we could talk a professor's secretary into letting us use her electric model when she was at lunch or on a break.

Typewriters and I never really got along very well. I could submit a term paper that weighed at least ten pounds and still only use two sheets of paper. The excess weight was created by typewriter correction fluid. That stuff saved me by covering my many typing errors. On the downside, I often ended up inhaling enough fumes to result in sentences along the lines of, "The American Civil War was the turning point in gee my fingers are really big aren't they?"

Brad doesn't have to worry about using correction fluid. He has spell check in the word processing system he uses. He has had varying results with that feature. He is the one who made it necessary for his mother and I to visit one of his teachers after he let spell check correct his misspelling of the word tentacles. The result was a sentence about alien beings attacking people with their ten-foot testicles.

The spell check feature is something that makes my columns at least partially understandable. I usually have a great many words that it wants to correct by the time I'm finished. It even tries to correct me on those occasional times that I have actually spelt something correctly. When Peder sent me the e-mail this morning about all the things today's freshmen have no recollection of experiencing in their lives, I wrote back that it was enough to make me drink a bottle of Geritol®. Spell check tried to change it to indicate that I was planning on drinking a bottle of genitals. I think that would have given Peder reason to have some severe doubts about what West Coast living had done to the guy he was best man for so many years ago.

Brad has the Internet to do his research. He can sit in his room hooked up to his computer while listening to music. I had a library filled with stern little old ladies whose sole job description seemed to involve shushing anyone who dared ask a question out loud. I tried to communicate with one of them by using the bit of sign language I knew and that just got me ejected from the building.

The list that the folks at Beloit College produced pointed out that today's freshmen didn't experience the Vietnam War era, the Front de la Liberation du Québec blowing up mailboxes in Canada, or Watergate blowing up faith in politicians everywhere. They were too young to remember the day Challenger exploded. Worse, they've never had the experience of having an ice-cold soft drink in their hands and not being able to find a bottle opener, because they've grown up in a twist-top world.

I think I'd like to trade places.

My Best Friend Is A Dog,
She Just Doesn't Know It

MY DOG'S NOT STUPID,
SHE HAS CANINE COGNITIVE DYSFUNCTION

Amazing.

All along I've thought the dog was just stupid. In fact, I usually refer to her as the dumbest dog to ever get lost on a single flight of stairs. It turns out she's not stupid after all. She apparently has a condition that veterinarians refer to as Canine Cognitive Dysfunction. It doesn't change the fact that she has the intelligence of a burlap sack full of rusty nails. In a way, I guess it's more politically correct to say she suffers from Canine Cognitive Dysfunction than calling her dumber than dirt.

The article I read about this condition said that it can strike dogs as young as seven-years-old. They must be talking in dog years, because Nipper has never shown herself to be anything but cognitively dysfunctional. The list of typical symptoms proves it:

<u>Housetraining Mishaps</u> — When Pavlov rang his bell his dog would drool. When anyone rings our bell, Nipper pees. Same concept, different end of the dog.

<u>Confusion or Disorientation</u> — Some people don't believe me when I say she gets lost on a single flight of stairs. I swear it's true. She gets halfway up and forgets where she is or where she is going. She must have learned the old adage about staying put if you get lost in the woods. Nipper will stay on the stairs until she

hears someone, then assumes that she must have been on her way to see them when she got lost.

Sleeping More During The Day — This is a moot point. I'm not sure if it's possible for this dog to sleep more during the day than she already does. Most days are spent sleeping on the couch or in the middle of my bed. She is incapable of cognitively discerning the words, "Get off of there." The only other example of a living being that can spend so much time asleep can also be found in our home. I'm sure, if we let him, my son would only arise from his slumber long enough to empty the refrigerator and say, "There's never any food in this house."

Awake More At Night — Normally, having the dog awake at night might be considered a good thing. She could act as a deterrent to robbers, by announcing their arrival. In Nipper's case, though, she doesn't like to be awake alone, and I seem to be the one with whom she wants to share her conscious moments. I cannot count the number of times I've woken up from a dream about cavorting along a tropical beach with a supermodel because of that dog. It can be quite disconcerting to discover that behind those artificially inflated supermodel lips lurks the aroma of dog breath. When my eyes and brain become accustomed to the light, and to being conscious at 3:00 AM, I find that I am face to snout with the dog, who appears to be saying, "Uhh . . . Gord . . . I couldn't sleep. Wanna go out back and pee on all the fence posts . . . Don't close your eyes Gord. If you do, I'll snort in your ear. Come on . . . It'll be a blast . . . Okay . . . here's a thought . . . Stay with me on this, Gordo . . . I'll go pee on the fence posts and you just stand at the door in your underwear in case I get lost . . . Okay, Gord . . . Gord . . . Uhh . . . Hey Gordo . . . Snort!"

Inappropriate Vocalization — She seems to believe it is her duty to give a running play-by-play of anything that is happening during her waking minutes. "Arf! Arf! Arf!" (There's a cat on the lawn.) "Yip. Bark! Woof!" Someone is walking on the sidewalk. "Whine! Whimper! Snort!" (Whatever it is you're eating, I'd like some, too.) The closest she comes to using inappropriate language is, "Yelp! Whimper! Arf! Yip! Arf! (Holy crap, he's lighting the barbecue . . . we're all gonna die . . . run for it.) It's surprisingly similar to what my wife says at the same time.

Shaking or Tremors — Her shaking is at its worst whenever anyone is eating. She can reach a wiggling frenzy that can be measured on the Richter scale if the food being consumed is pizza. If she feels that the person eating the subject of her desire is not getting the message, she starts throwing in some Inappropriate Vocalization (see Whine! Whimper! Snort! Above.) The "Whine" and the "Whimper!" aren't so bad. It's the "Snort!" that really grabs your attention — especially if you're wearing shorts.

In a way, it's comforting to know that there is a medical reason for the complete lack of brainpower exhibited by the dog in my life. 'Cognitive Dysfunction' sounds so much better than 'Stupid'.

Perhaps I can use the term for other, otherwise-known-as-stupid, events that seem to occur all too frequently around here. Just think how much nicer it will be to say, "Son, it was cognitively dysfunctional of you to paint your school project on the new carpets." Even better, I can now say, "Oh, cognitively dysfunctional me, I've locked the keys in the car . . . again."

Someone told me the other day that it costs a dollar a day to keep a pet. That means that I'm putting out over $1,000 a year, and I'm not sure that I am getting my money's worth from any of them.

I'm sure that if anyone ever hooked my dog up to one of those machines that reads brain waves, they would immediately classify her as an organ donor. Her only cognitive thoughts occur when she sees food, smells food, or hears me making food.

Judging by the way she gulps down anything that is given to her, or that accidentally gets dropped from the kitchen counter, she rarely, if ever, has to use the part of her brain that would normally register the sense of taste.

This dog is very easily confused. Ninety-nine point nine percent of the time she goes in and out through the kitchen door — usually tripping the person who has opened the door in the first place.

If you're going out, then she has to go out there with you. If you're going in you might be getting something to eat, so she's there to trip you on the way back, too.

The problem arises if you decide to go out through another door. She bolts through, just as fast as ever, but suddenly realizes that she's not outside the kitchen door. The dog will immediately start running in a tight circle, barking at the top of her lungs in a panic-stricken eruption of sound. I think it translates into, "Hey, wait a second. We're not outside the kitchen. Oh no! We're lost! We're lost. How will I ever find my way back to my food dish? How could you do this to us? We're both gonna die out here? Help! Help! Help!"

If you let her back in the house, she gives a momentary look that says, "Oh, thank goodness. You found our way back into the house," followed by another eruption and more running in circles. "Oh no we aren't in the kitchen. Where's my food dish? You've gone and gotten us lost in the dining room now. Help! Help! Help!"

Most dogs are able to master the concept of fetch. Mine loves having someone throw a tennis ball for her. She runs after it, grabs it, and then lies down with it and chews it until it's turned into something no one would ever want to touch again.

If she gets bored, or perhaps if she starts to get disgusted by the slobbery ball, she might return with it, and drop it on the first pair of bare feet she encounters. By then the ball is twice its previous weight because of the sheer volume of dog spit it has absorbed. Hence, a game of fetch with this dog rarely gets past the opening pitch of the season.

The oldest cat, the one abandoned here by the son who recently moved out, has two speeds 'Do we need to check to see if she's still breathing,' and 'She's meowing so she must want someone to pick her up and carry her to her food dish.' I've often been tempted to check the *Guinness Book of Records* to see if they have a category for least exertion of energy by a cat.

The youngest cat is the biggest problem of the three animal freeloaders around here. She expends more energy than the other two put together. Unfortunately, most of it is spent causing trouble. She behaves like a puma trapped in the body of a house cat. She's one of those cats who will chase anything that moves — especially if it's a body part under the blankets.

Because I am not a morning person, it's usually my body parts that get attacked. My wife leaves the bedroom door open when she gets up in the morning, giving the cat tacit permission to attack whatever part of me might move. I've learned the hard way to lie very still and protect any particularly sensitive areas as soon as I hear the door open in the morning.

I've also learned the hard way to make sure that cat isn't in the room when I am drying myself after a shower. She'll attack anything that jiggles under the towel. At my size, there is usually a whole lot of jiggling going on, but then, you didn't want to think about that did you?

Now that I have a clearer picture of what these animals are costing me, they'd better be on their toes. For ninety dollars a month, I expect a lot more respect than the cats give me, and I really don't think I should be expected to rescue a lost dog from the stairway every couple of hours.

My friend Blaine has been shelling out money by the fistful to veterinarians lately. His golden retriever has probably cost him several thousand dollars this month because of two or three ruptured disks in his spine. This same dog went through another pile of money last year at this time when it lost a leg to cancer.

There are those who would say, "But it's just a dog . . . " Anyone who says that should never be allowed the luxury of sharing their home with a dog, because there is no such thing as "just-a-dog."

Dogs earn the right to be part of the family just by being in the house. They don't eat nearly as much as teenage sons. They don't ask to borrow the car. They don't even expect you to drop everything to drive them to their girlfriend's house.

Over the years I have shared my life with a variety of animals. There have probably been about twenty that have looked at me as their source of food and shelter, and that doesn't even count my two sons.

These days, the dog job-shares her pet duties with two cats of undetermined parentage. The older one belongs to my oldest son, who moved out when he went to college. As a result, his cat has decided to adopt me. It spends most of the day trying to get my attention away from the computer by climbing up on my lap and preventing me from seeing the keyboard. The fact that she weighs about sixteen pounds means that climbing on my lap usually involves embedding her claws into my thigh before attempting to hoist herself up. This usually results in a significant blood loss on my part. A couple of weeks ago, she was trying to climb up onto the back of my chair when she started to slip. She caught herself by inserting a claw into my ear. I think people in Bolivia heard me scream.

The dog has been around for the last twelve years. She is by no means the first dumb dog I have owned. One of the more memorable was a huge brute of a dog that was part husky and part Newfoundland. When we took him to obedience lessons he was the best dog in the class. Unfortunately, he forgot everything he learned by the time he got back to the car.

This dog had a Houdini-like ability to get off his leash. Once, a neighboring farmer came to our door announcing that he would shoot our dog if it came near his chickens again. The next day the farmer was back, shotgun in hand, accusing the dog of once again treating himself to some take-out chicken. I was sure he was tied to a tree in the backyard, but his alibi was lost when he slowly came around the corner of the house with a feather sticking out of his mouth like a toothpick. We managed to get the death sentence reprieved by offering to find the dog another home far away from our neighbor's chickens.

Another dog of mine that suffered from cranial dysfunction was a cross between a Labrador retriever and an Irish setter. Its Labrador lineage would tend to indicate that it did indeed have a brain, but the setter in him meant that the brain was not attached to anything important. The only way this dog could stop when he ran down the hill behind our house was to career full force into the back door.

Perhaps all of these dogs appear to be a few kibbles short of a bowlful because of the one smart dog we owned for thirteen years. He was a border collie and nothing short of brilliant. Comparing him to all of our other pets would be similar to comparing Einstein to a hockey puck. His biggest shortcoming was his habit of stealing any bottle of beer left within his reach. He never learned the correlation between drinking beer and his outbursts of severe flatulence.

Despite all of their shortcomings, none of the dogs I have ever owned could be called "just a dog," at least not in my presence. Dogs, and even cats, whether brainless or brilliant, drunkards or chicken thieves, accept us unconditionally.

I just wish the one around here could make it up the stairs without getting lost.

A Dumb Dog Is One Thing, A Clumsy Dumb Dog Is Quite Another

The dog has had a tough couple of weeks. She had some minor surgery, which, in itself, was disconcerting enough for her limited cognitive abilities. The real strain on her mental capacity came with the collar she had to wear to keep her from licking the stitches. Not only did it completely baffle her, it made her look like Space Dog From The Planet Phydough. I'm almost certain that if we could have gotten her to sit still long enough she could have been used as a dish to watch satellite TV.

She's been walking around the house in more of a daze than usual because the collar completely eliminates her peripheral vision. As a result, she has been bumping into furniture, walls, and people with virtually every step she's taken. In the ten days that she's been wearing the thing she hasn't yet figured out that she has to adjust the amount of room she needs to get past something.

We've put up with her stupidity for over twelve years. Adding incredible clumsiness to her diminished brainpower has been hard to take. She follows me around the house on the chance that I might be doing something that involves food. I can never be more than a couple of steps ahead of her. Wearing her space helmet/satellite dish severely reduces her ability to stop in time. She's developed a habit of bumping into me, just behind my knees with her space helmet. I have enough trouble staying upright on my crutches without having my knees pushed out of joint every time I stop too quickly for her to avoid rear-ending me.

Her collar also has a negative impact on my ability to get a decent night's sleep. She has a habit of sneaking up onto the end of our bed after we fall asleep. She then spends the night competing with my wife for my share of the blankets. Her collar makes it difficult to sneak anywhere. It catches on the mattress whenever she tries to jump onto the bed. As a result, she has to make several attempts before she finally makes it onto the bed. Sleeping through that performance is impossible.

Falling back asleep is also very difficult. Her reduced peripheral vision makes it hard for her to judge where the side of the bed is. As a result, every night has been a continuous cycle of trying to jump onto the bed, falling off, and trying to jump back up again.

Next to getting lost on the stairs, this dog's best skill is eating. I think she prides herself on her ability to consume whatever is available. Dropped food rarely gets a chance to bounce off the floor before it's devoured. It took her quite a while to figure out how to eat and drink while wearing the collar. If she approached her bowl in a normal fashion, the collar hit the edge before her mouth could reach the contents. I'm actually quite amazed that a dog of her intellectual capability was able to determine that she had to bend her neck to the point that the collar encircled the bowl. The only problem with that method was that it became dark inside the collar and she couldn't see her food.

Navigating a flight of stairs has always been hard enough for this dog. The only chance she has to make it from one end to the other without falling is if she can watch her front paws and hope that the rear ones stay synchronized. The collar cut off her view of her feet. Straining to catch a glimpse of her toes meant keeping the collar on a severe angle. As a result, the collar kept catching on the steps. Three times last week I heard her barrel roll down the last half of the stairs after her attempts at keeping the whole process coordinated became too much for her.

She finally got the stitches removed yesterday. The disappearance of the collar will make her life a lot easier, but it will also eliminate a lot of perfectly good excuses for her behavior. It'll just be her own innate dumbness to blame the next time she falls down the stairs.

It won't be the collar's fault when she wakes us up in the middle of the night falling off the bed. Her low IQ will now be the only culprit when she misjudges the depth of her water dish and she has to spend twenty minutes sneezing and snorting water out of her sinuses.

If nothing else, she's good entertainment.

It's been quite a day. It's 9:00 PM and I am just now sitting down to write this week's column, something I normally do first thing in the morning on my deadline day. On a day like today, I might be tempted to tell the editors to rerun an old column or get my 800 words written with a whole mess of "La la, la la la la, la la la la la . . . ," except with my luck I'd run afoul of copyright law for plagiarizing the theme from *The Smurfs*.

Today was spent dealing with an appearance on a nationally televised talk show. I'm used to doing TV and radio shows, but today's was more than a little bit unusual, stressful, and downright chaotic. It was the television debut of Nipper, the dumbest dog to ever get lost on a single flight of stairs.

The producers had seen a picture of Nipper and me on the front page of the Vancouver newspaper when it was announced that my first book, *Justice Is Blind — And Her Dog Just Peed In My Cornflakes*, was one of five finalists for the Leacock Medal. In the picture Nipper was licking my face, and looking almost like a dog that came equipped with a functioning cerebellum. What people looking at that picture don't know is that in order to get the picture I endured twenty minutes of sitting on the floor with peanut butter spread on my cheek. We went through nearly a cup of peanut butter before the photographer was satisfied. I still shudder when I think about the number of times the she missed my cheek and licked my tonsils.

Clearly the producers had either lost their minds or they really didn't know what to expect from Nipper. Frankly, I wasn't sure what to expect just trying to get her to the studio. She is not a car dog. I think she associates cars with getting needles at the vet's so she cries the entire time we drive her anywhere. The twenty-five mile drive to the TV station was probably the most time she had ever spent in a car. Her state of hysteria reached a pinnacle when I pulled into the parking garage. It was almost as if she was saying, "Holy crap, Gord, you've gone and driven right into a building. We're probably both going to die. If we survive this you're not going to stick the blame on me."

The next piece of excitement came when we got into an elevator. She was startled when it began to move. Let's just say I wouldn't want to be the next person to get on that elevator.

When you are waiting for your turn to go on, you sit in what's known as the green room. I've been in dozens of green rooms, but for some reason, I've never been in one that is green. Today's green room was orange. The green room usually has comfortable chairs, a TV to watch the other segments of the show being taped, and food. Nipper and I went into a separate room from the rest of the guests. Ostensibly, this was to help calm her down. Truthfully, it was to keep her out of reach of the tray full of bagels.

It didn't work.

The sliding door between the rooms was slightly ajar. Her ability to open that door and attack the bagel tray only proves that she does more thinking with her stomach than she does with her brain.

The highlight of the day came when I had to go to makeup. Nipper doesn't like to be left alone. She doesn't keep her feelings to herself.

She howls.

Loudly.

She howled so loudly that the guest rock band taping their segment of the show at the time had to stop and redo their song.

Twice.

She really surprised me when they brought her onto the set to join me at the end of my appearance. She enjoyed the audience and they enjoyed her. She actually acted like a seemingly intelligent, well-mannered dog about town. Go figure . . .

The old girl is asleep at my feet now. Every so often she twitches, perhaps remembering the horrors of her master driving right into a building, that little room that moved all by itself, or being left alone in the green room. Occasionally, she opens her eyes and heaves a huge sigh. When she does, an unusual aroma fills the air. It's a combination of dog-breath mixed with cinnamon-raison and garlic-onion bagels.

She definitely needs a breath mint . . .

. . . or fifty.

Maybe I shouldn't say anything. Perhaps it isn't something that I should mention in such a public forum, but I'm troubled.

I'm more than a bit concerned about all of the changes I'm starting to see in her. After so many years together it's come as a bit of a surprise, although I guess at her age I should have been expecting it to start soon. They, whoever "they" are, say that it's just a natural part of life.

I started to notice it more when she seemed to be tired so much of the time. These days, sitting in the living room after dinner, she can hardly keep her eyes open. Often it's a struggle just to get any kind of a response from her. She'll take a pass on things she used to enjoy, wanting only to hit the sack early.

It's just as bad in the morning. The alarm used to wake her up and she'd be anxious to get her day started. Now there is scarcely any movement from her after three, four, and sometimes even five, alarms. Some mornings I've been so worried about her that I've actually checked to see if she is still breathing.

In her younger days she was quite an avid runner. At times it seemed that she was totally consumed by a desire to run. Today I think she'd be hard pressed to run more than a few strides before returning to what has become her slow, almost labored, stride. Given her choice between running, walking, and just sleeping on the couch, she'd take the couch option ten times out of ten.

It isn't just her lack of energy that I've been noticing. She's changing in other ways, too. For example, and I realize that it might be a bit indiscreet to mention it, but she is really troubled lately by gas. Believe me, when she's troubled by gas problems everybody in the immediate vicinity is going to be troubled by her gas. It's gotten so bad that I ordered a free sample of Beano$^®$ off the Internet the other day that I'm going to try to slip into her dinner to see if it improves things a bit.

It's starting to cause me a lot of embarrassment. She didn't think anyone would notice the other day when she slipped with a little eruption on the elevator in our building. Wouldn't you know it, when we got off at the parking level, there was someone waiting to get on the elevator. What could I do? Tell her that she'd be better advised to take the stairs? The woman probably thinks I did it, because the elevator certainly didn't have a very ladylike aroma. I can only hope she noticed that I was trying to hold my breath as I got off the elevator and thinks my pained expression and the smell was the result of someone who got off on the ground floor.

Her hearing isn't what it used to be either. It seems that I have to be looking right at her or she doesn't even know I'm talking to her. A few times when we've been out together lately, I've had to make a lot of noise and start walking in another direction just to get her attention.

Her memory isn't serving her to well these days, either. That's not to say that it was particularly anything to marvel at in her younger years. You'd think that once she had followed the same route a couple of times she could remember how to get from point A to point B without too much difficulty. Without a lot of my help she'd be lost more often than she'd know where she is.

I guess I should be thankful for all of the good years we've had together. At her age I guess I should be willing to overlook these signs of aging and rejoice in each day we have remaining together. In fact, I guess I have to admit that the years have taken their toll on me, too. I'm certainly not the same man I was when she came into my life. I probably enjoy sleeping more now, too. I'm definitely a lot slower when we go for a walk together. Still, it saddens me when I think that we may not have as many years ahead of us as we do behind us.

In reality it could be a lot worse. I could have been writing this piece about my wife instead of my dog. I'd be in a lot of trouble if I said things like that about my wife.

I may be crazy, but I'm not stupid.

It hasn't been a fun week. This is a column that I knew would eventually have to be written, but no matter how prepared you might think you are for inevitable events, they still throw you for a loop when they occur.

Anyone who has read this column over the past seven years has gotten to know one of my regular characters. People have often wondered if Nipper, the dumbest dog to ever get lost on a single flight of stairs, was real or imaginary. She's been a real part of my life for over thirteen years.

On Friday, August 31, 2001, Nipper passed away. She'd had a stroke just after I filed a column about how lucky I considered myself to be lately. Perhaps I tempted fate a bit with that column. I don't feel nearly as lucky today. Over the course of the thirty-six hours she survived after the stroke, she slowly lost her vision, and her walking was severely impaired. For the first time since she was a puppy, she peed on the carpet, although the tile at the front door was often dampened if someone rang the doorbell.

I spent all that night sitting up with her. She lay on the couch beside me with her head on my lap. Several times throughout the night I thought she was slipping away. In the morning I took her to see her vet, but before he could see her, she slipped away on my lap in his waiting room.

Nipper used to get her own fan mail from my readers, so I know it wasn't just my life or the lives of my family members who she touched over the years.

No, she was not a brilliant dog. Her best trick was her impersonation of Tim Allen grunting for pizza crusts. Her passing hasn't made much of a difference to the intelligence of the planet. What she lacked in brainpower, she more than compensated for with her ability to love unconditionally. She tried to be friends with everyone she met. Human, canine, feline, it didn't matter to her. I'm just glad she never met a skunk because she would have tried to make friends with it, too. Skunks don't make good buddies. Our first dog learned that lesson the hard way.

My office seems like a quiet, lonely, and desolate place this week. Working, as I do from home, Nipper and I spent several hours together each day. Much of the time she would be asleep under my desk with her favorite cushion. Occasionally, she would wake up and realize that it was time to get me to stop working and smell the dog biscuits. She could become quite vocal if she thought I was ignoring the opportunity to give her a treat. More than one newspaper editor has wondered what the racket in the background was when she let me know it was time for a biscuit break and I happened to be on the telephone.

Recently a Japanese company announced a new product that would translate your dog's moods by the noises the animal made. I believe that anyone who needs something like that to translate dog into English shouldn't be allowed to have a pet. I've often written about Nipper's various vocalizations and how clear she was when she used them. Looking over some of those old columns about her this week has reminded me a great deal about how much and what I loved about her.

Perhaps her most famous vocal attempts were the ones she'd use when we lived in a house with a staircase. She would regularly get halfway up the stairs and forgot either where she was going, or how to get there. I'd often have to come to her rescue when I'd hear the collection of barks and grunts that clearly meant, "Uhh, Gord . . . I'm lost again . . . I'm on that bumpy part of the floor . . . Every time I take a step there is another bump in the floor in front of me just like the last one . . . Can I get to my supper dish from here . . . ? Gord . . . Hey! Gord . . . "

She also had a unique vocabulary that she brought out whenever I tried to light the barbecue. She'd run in circles and loudly yip what could only mean, "Oh Geez . . . He's trying to set fire to the meat again . . . Don't do it Gord. Let's just eat it raw . . . You're gonna kill us with that gas barbecue one of these days." She learned that one from my wife.

Nipper gave me a lot to laugh about and a lot to love in her thirteen and a half years. Even though that is supposedly the equivalent to ninety-something in human years, it was far too short a lifetime.

Goodbye, Old Girl. I'm really going to miss you.

Life Is Strange —
And I Do My Part To Keep It That Way

I used to think thirty was old. Like most people under that age in the late Sixties, I believed the advice that one should never trust anyone over thirty. I thought it must be a terrible thing to find that you're facing that age.

As time went on I came to realize that turning thirty wasn't so bad. In fact, I sailed through my thirtieth birthday fairly easily, still feeling young and somewhat vibrant. At the time, I thought I still had at least five years before age would catch up to me sometime around my thirty-fifth birthday. Five years still felt like a long time then.

Those five years went by pretty quickly, and I came to the conclusion that thirty-five wasn't such a bad age, either. Heck, I was only halfway to seventy, and just twice the age I was when I first met my wife. I knew there were clouds on the horizon, though. After all, forty was fast approaching, and it was a generally accepted fact that forty was the point when you were officially over the hill.

Just as everyone who is twenty-nine dreads the thought of thirty, those who have reached thirty-nine don't want to think about forty. My generation grew up with Jack Benny on television. No matter how old he was, he would only admit to a perpetual thirty-nine.

That image seemed to stick with us all. When I hit thirty-nine I could understand why Jack Benny didn't want to age any further. Forty really did seem like a barrier. What came before it was youthful enthusiasm. The other side of the wall looked like impending geriatrics.

As the pre-forty days drifted past, I was quite surprised how easy the transition was. Forty wasn't so bad. I didn't go through any sort of caterpillar-like transformation that saw me wake up one morning with an overwhelming desire for Sinatra, prunes, and sensible shoes. I could still listen to rock and roll. My bodily functions seemed to continue functioning without the aid of dehydrated fruit, and my cowboy boots were still the most comfortable shoes I'd ever found.

I started a new life at forty. My first newspaper column appeared that year. I started getting things back on track at forty. The accident that left me disabled happened just before I turned thirty-seven, and, while I hated hearing doctors suggest that I 'learn to live with it,' I discovered that, by forty, I really had started to learn to live with it. Forty was fun. Writing had always been a dream, and now I was doing something that I had wanted to do when I was twenty, and I was even getting paid to do it.

Clearly, I didn't have time to feel my age at forty. I came to the conclusion that I wouldn't have to feel old until I turn forty-eight.

I just turned forty-eight . . .

When I looked in the mirror this morning, the face that stared back at me was clearly a lot older than the ones that were reflected at twenty, thirty, thirty-five, thirty-nine, and forty. My hair and beard are now predominantly gray. Far more so than at this time last year if my publicity pictures are the judge. My youngest son is now the age I was when I got married. He's at that point in life when he is convinced that the geriatric ward is for people over thirty. Parts of me don't work as well as they once did. I need three separate pairs of glasses, and though I hate to admit it, I've given in to the need for a magnifying glass if I really want to read the newspaper's stock market report.

Still, all things considered, I've reached this milestone without feeling old yet. I guess that comes later than I thought. Maybe it's fifty I should be worried about, but that's only two years away, so I think I should put the bar a little further out of reach. Perhaps I can start giving in and accepting my antiquity when I'm fifty-five or sixty. No matter when it happens, it will be made considerably easier by the fact that my wife has gotten there six months before me.

On the other hand, I might never have to feel old. I can accept the fact that my date of birth is getting further and further away from my birthday every year. So what if I'm a bit older, I can still go on just like I always have.

I can get older every day, but I don't have to ever grow up.

I've just returned from spending ten days camping. Sometime during the second or third day I reached the point when I had been roughing it for too long. I missed my television, my microwave, and I had started sending postcards to Mr. Coffee®.

During the first couple of days of a camping trip, most people feel invigorated by the fresh air, the sights and sounds of nature, and the sense of adventure. During the final couple days of a camping trip they feel a kinship to prisoners of war. Over the course of the last two weeks I have been at both ends of that spectrum. There's something about serving as a walking buffet for every kind of biting and stinging insect known to man that can take the wonder out of nature.

Looking back I can see I missed a number of clear warning signs that might have given me a clue that I'd been camping too long. They were all subtle little things that, taken on their own, might not have raised much alarm, but when grouped into the entire experience, were a clear indication that I had been away from my orthopedic mattress for too many nights.

For those of you who may be contemplating a camping trip in the near future, I have compiled a list that you should pin to the wall of your tent. Don't worry about rain coming in through the pinholes. Once it starts raining, the water will come in through a hundred other places and pool beneath your last pair of clean underwear, so an extra pinhole or two won't make much of a difference.

You've been camping too long when:
• You have mosquito bites in places that your doctor would need special instruments to examine.
• You find several hundred ants holding an Olympic-style swimming event in the melted ice in your cooler.
• You start recognizing your fellow campers by the sight of their shoes under a restroom stall door.
• You start to wonder how many toes you'd need to cut off before they would airlift you out of there.
• Skunks are repulsed by your smell.
• You know the words to all the songs on your neighbor's cassette collection of Serbo-Croatian folk songs.
• You'd be willing to trade in your Greenpeace membership for a shotgun to take out the birds that insist on singing right outside your tent at 4:30 AM.
• The Forest Service water bomber is called in to extinguish your propane camp stove — for the third time.
• You start to size up the kindling potential of your neighbor's guitar.
• You've given names to all of the spiders in the three closest outhouses.
• You forget what eggs taste like when they aren't covered in a layer of campfire ash.
• The game warden declares the little trench you dug around your tent to be a viable fish habitat.

- Even though the blond in the next campsite is wearing a micro-thong, it's too much effort to keep your eyes open.
- The initials someone carved on your picnic table seat are permanently outlined on your butt.
- You stop worrying about rattlesnakes and think of them as a possible way to get you into a nice comfortable bed in the emergency room.
- You stop dividing your clothes into bags marked "Clean" and "Dirty" and start sorting them into "Dirty" and "Unbelievably Filthy."
- You offer another camper one hundred dollars for her roll of two-ply toilet paper, only to be outbid by the owner of the campground.
- You find mutant mosquitoes drinking your bottle of insect repellent.
- You try shampooing your hair in a thunderstorm.
- You're getting used to eating food that's charred on the outside and raw in the middle.
- You wake up with a headache and a backache, but that's the best you feel all day.
- Your air mattress has more patches than Microsoft® Windows®.
- You've developed a better relationship with the bloodsuckers in the lake than the ones back at the office.
- You convince yourself that coveting your neighbor's luxury motor home is not the same thing as the commandment against coveting your neighbor's ass.
- You start making a list of all the ways to tell you've been camping too long.

As John Denver sang, "Gee, it's good to be back home again."

I'm not a big fan of February. Its only redeeming quality is that it only lasts twenty-eight or twenty-nine days. Unfortunately, February's dominant characteristics make it seem like it lasts twenty-eight or twenty-nine weeks.

Here in Canada, it's right in the middle of the longest stretch without a holiday. After New Year's Day, we don't see another long weekend until Easter. In that period, my American readers get Martin Luther King Jr. Day, and Presidents Day, which combines Lincoln's and Washington's birthdays. That's what I get for living in a country that doesn't assassinate a leader every so often.

Even Valentine's Day can't save February. Oh sure, any excuse to indulge in chocolate hearts has a certain appeal to it, but for most men, it's a day we know we'd better not forget, and a day we'd just as soon not remember. Forgetting Valentine's Day would be worse than forgetting Christmas. If our wives, or significant others, know that we love them the other 364 days a year, why do they need us to buy candy that they say they're trying to avoid eating, at least until the candy they ate at Christmas has been worked off their hips? They also expect us to go out and buy a card that expresses our deepest feelings.

Most men aren't even sure how to express their shallow feelings.

We stand in little shops staring at cards that use flowery, sentimental words, most of us would never use in our day-to-day conversation.

Of course, how could we let Valentine's Day slip by without remembering her with flowers? Who came up with that idea? It's the middle of winter for Pete's sake. How many flowers are in season? Those that are available cost three times as much as they would in, say, July, but just try slipping your true love a rain check for a dozen roses to be delivered next July. Chances are, you'll never have to redeem it. Your true love will have traded you in for someone who will venture into a florist's shop in February, credit card in hand.

It's not even our fault. Valentine's Day just wasn't a highpoint for boys when we were kids. Most of us went to school on Valentine's Day with a cutout card for every member of the class, even the ones we didn't like, because our mothers made us treat everyone equally. Who among us didn't spend the day fearing that the only cutout cards we'd get were from the other kids with mothers like ours? Even worse, we feared that some girl might actually take this 'be my Valentine' stuff seriously.

The absolute worst thing that could happen to us on Valentine's Day was to actually have one of our friends see us slip a card onto a girl's desk. If we were lucky the razzing we'd take might abate by St. Patrick's Day. Of course, the only joy the day brought us was the possibility of spotting one of our friends playing postman at a girl's desk. It was so much more fun to be a razzer than a razzee.

It seems that February is also the month that traditionally has the worst weather. When I was a kid, living in Ontario, it brought us extra snow shoveling duties. On the good side, it occasionally brought enough snow to close the schools, but unless you are a student or a teacher, that benefit is pretty moot. Now that I live on the West Coast, February means rain. I'm not positive, but I firmly believe that all the hammering and sawing I keep hearing is one of my neighbors building an ark.

A couple of weeks ago, one of my readers sent me a note asking what colour the sky is in my world. I think it might be a veiled reference to my questionable sanity at times. Unfortunately, gray clouds have blocked it out for so long, I can't remember the last time I saw the green sun or purple sky.

Face it. We'd all be better off if we just hibernated through the whole month.

This seems to be the time of year for telethons. Every charitable institution from PBS to The Society for the Prevention of Cruelty to Reform Party Members jumps on the bandwagon and runs a twenty-four-hour televised event hoping to raise money and awareness of their plight. One recent telethon in my area took in over $5 million for children's charities. Obviously, that is the sort of thing worth supporting.

I'm less inclined to contribute to the two separate PBS channels that I get on my cable, just so that I can watch the *Antiques Roadshow* in two different time zones. One, maybe, but there is only so much airtime dedicated to Mr. Rogers putting on his shoes that I can see myself supporting.

What about all the worthy causes that don't get telethons? I think it's time that the broadcasting conglomerates started donating airtime to less well-known problems in society that could use the kind of financial windfall a telethon might bring.

Parents of Adolescents Needing Increased Consumables (P.A.N.I.C.) could hold a telethon to help ease the financial burden on parents of teenagers. For example they could raise money to:

• Help pay for additional telephone lines so that parents could actually use the phone while their children are on the Internet, talking to their boyfriends or girlfriends, or waiting for a call more important than anything that parents might need it for

• Provide financial assistance to parents whose sons and daughters are graduating from high school, and therefore need a constant flow of money to cover graduation photographs, school rings, tuxedo rentals, gown purchases, limo rentals, and grad party tickets

• Reimburse parents for all the empty gas tanks that their teenagers promised faithfully would be filled if they could use the car

• Pay for towing to the nearest gas station when a parent, believing that their teenager had refilled the gas tank, runs out of gas on the freeway during rush hour when they are late for a meeting

• Provide emergency food rations when a teenager wipes out a week's groceries during a 1:00 AM feeding frenzy.

One's mid-forties seem to be the time when the mail brings invitations to weddings, bridal showers, and baby showers for the children of friends and relations. A telethon for Getting Invited to Frequent Trendy Showers (G.I.F.T.S.) would raise money to help defray the costs of attending all of these events. This is especially important now that showers have become specialized events. My wife recently attended a shower for the daughter of a friend of ours that focused entirely on products for use in the bedroom. No, it wasn't sheets and pillowcases. The array of gifts would have made a West Hollywood hooker blush.

Closely related is another charity that could really use a telethon to raise the kind of money needed to ease the financial burden for potentially destitute and downtrodden citizens. Wedding Expenses Drained Dad's Entire Deposits (W.E.D.D.E.D.) could hold a telethon to help fathers whose daughters want them to pay for champagne weddings when they only have club soda bank accounts.

Unfortunately, some people become financially incapable of keeping up with ever-changing computer technology. Owners of High-end Computers Requiring Astronomical Payments (O.H.C.R.A.P.) could explore the option of running a telethon to help its members survive without the latest technology until they finish paying for their last computer purchase. The money would be used to provide members with massive doses of Prozac to help them deal with depression and processor envy.

I could really use some help from an organization like F.R.O.S.T. (Families Residing with Overheated Spouses' Thermostats) A telethon could help it purchase thermal underwear, sweaters, and flannel-lined clothing for family members living with women experiencing frequent hot flashes. Existing telethons raise money to pay for specially trained dogs to assist the blind or mobility impaired. Perhaps F.R.O.S.T. could purchase St. Bernard puppies and train them to help the non-thermally overachieving members of a family ward off hypothermia.

On the other side of the coin, Spouses of Husbands with Immature Tendencies (we won't bother with the acronym here) could hold a telethon to help wives whose husbands, in a vain attempt to retain their youth, drain joint bank accounts in order to pay for sports cars, hair implants, and line dancing lessons.

Since it's doubtful that we will ever see telethons for causes like these, I'll be happy to accept your donations and make sure they are given to a worthy, fifty-year-old columnist who is:

• a father of children with large appetites

• has friends and relations whose kids are getting married, having babies or housewarming parties

• has a computer prone to occasional bouts of cyber-Alzheimer's

• banned from setting the thermostat in the house or car.

I guess you could call it a perverse sort of pleasure, but I'm always happy when one of my friends does something that shows he's advancing in age, while I still have a bit more time to feel younger. My hair has gone quite gray, and my wife, who is much older than I am (Okay, it's only five and a half months but I just like pointing it out as often as possible), still only has a couple strands of gray. So any opportunity to feel young needs to be relished to its fullest extent.

My buddy Wayne recently became a grandfather. Imagine that. He has two generations directly beneath him on his family tree, while I am still luxuriating in the smug glow of having only one. I've told my sons that I will be quite happy to delay the addition of another generation to my lineage for a few more years, so that I can keep pointing out to Wayne that he must be a lot older than me.

Of course, it's pretty exciting to have a new baby around to spoil a bit. When young Dylan made his first visit to our place at the ripe old age of six days, he was the center of attention. Even my youngest son took a turn at holding him, although he calculated his comfort level perfectly, and handed him off to another set of willing arms just seconds before the baby had a chance to produce some baby byproducts in his diaper.

Like all parents, Wayne's daughter and son-in-law want the best for their new son. They have hand painted a floor-to-ceiling, wall-to-wall mural in his bedroom featuring all of the characters from the Disney version of *Winnie-the-Pooh*.

It's a far more impressive nursery than the one my first son came home to, although Pooh and his friends were that room's dominant features, too. I am not nearly as artistic as Tammy and Shawn. I put up wallpaper. The sheets were supposed to join at Pooh's left leg and Tigger's tail. They looked fine at the top of the wall, but by the time the pattern reached the floor it looked like Pooh had a compound fracture and Tigger had gotten his tail caught in a car door.

As with all things, we gain more knowledge about children's literature as time goes by. My wife and I might be excused for putting up *Winnie-the-Pooh* back in the dark ages around 1980, but I think Tammy and Shawn might have to consider repainting their nursery, based on recent information about the goings on in Hundred Acre Wood.

A group of doctors from Halifax published a paper in the *Canadian Medical Association Journal* that indicated Pooh's gang might not be the best role models for our children (and in Wayne's case, grandchildren). According to the paper, Pooh's constant focus on food and persistent counting are signs of an obsessive-compulsive disorder. He may have even been brain damaged when Christopher Robin, a child with numerous gender conflicts, dragged him down the stairs, "bump, bump, bump."

Piglet is in serious need of medication to control his panic attacks. Eeyore could definitely use a prescription for antidepressants. Owl, who spells his name Wol, is dyslexic. Tigger is hyperactive and has a propensity to take undo risks. In a comment worthy of Dan Quayle, the doctors pointed out all of the potential problems that could befall the single parent, Kanga, and her soon-to-be-juvenile-delinquent offspring Roo.

Taking this all a step further, there seems to be a major problem ahead for parents seeking to provide positive role models on the walls of their newborn's nurseries. Isn't Yogi Bear an obvious kleptomaniac with a lack of respect for authority figures like Mr. Ranger-Sir? Doesn't he seem to have a bit of an eating disorder, too? Do we want to expose week-old babies to the symbiotic relationship between the sadistic Road Runner and the masochistic Wile E. Coyote? Aren't both Donald and Daffy Duck in need of intensive anger management therapy?

Studies like this could ruin the careers of everyone from Bugs Bunny (another compulsive eating disorder) to Popeye (inability to make a long-term commitment to Olive). To say nothing of vicious aggressiveness of Tom and Jerry, or the cruelty to small animals displayed by Sylvester the Cat, a clear sign that he may be taking the first steps towards becoming a psychopathic serial killer.

I'm sure I know what Shawn would say to the idea of painting over Dylan's mural to save him from these potentially bad influences.

. . . and, no, it definitely wouldn't be, "Oh bother!"

There aren't many rooms in the average house that a man can lay claim to with any degree of confidence. I guess we should just be thankful that we get to live in what is supposed to be our castles. Assuming that our input into the household décor might be welcomed is about as naive as assuming that we might be asked for our input into the design features of the International Space Station.

For most men, the bathroom is one of those chambers-of-horror when it comes to selecting the décor. Left to us, it would have the obligatory standard equipment — tub, shower, sink, toilet, magazine rack, and beer cooler — and not much else. That's the sort of facility single men might have, but I doubt that many married men — or even many single men who from time to time may be visited by members of the opposite sex — could ever dream of owning.

Face it, for most men the bathroom is the modern-day version of the reading room. It's that little area of escape not offered elsewhere in the house. We should be able to go in, sit down, pull out a magazine, newspaper, or a book, and relax for a few minutes without the rest of the world encroaching on our reverie.

But do we get that?

Noooooooooooo . . .

Trying to enjoy that quiet time away from it all is made difficult by the accoutrements that feminize that room. How can any man feel at home sharing a room with a basketful of perfumed soaps right there behind him on the top of the toilet tank? The counter around the sink is no better. Makeup, hair products, and a myriad of other feminine stuff take up all of the usable space. I guess I should be thankful that there is a place for my toothbrush, even if it's only because the electric toothbrush holder came with room for two brushes.

Like most men, I put up with all of this feminization of the bathroom in the name of household peace, but this latest affront is just too much. My wife came into my office on the weekend with a newspaper article that she thought I should read. I sincerely hope she wasn't suggesting we buy the product described in the article.

It was about the resurgence of interest in bidets — those European devices that are supposed to provide your nether regions with a gentle, cleansing shower. I've been terrified about the concept of bidets ever catching on in North America since the wife of a friend of mine accidentally scalded her "sensitive body parts" on their wedding night when she tried out the bidet in their honeymoon suite.

The article Diane brought me focused on the development of a product for people who don't have room for a freestanding model. A Japanese company has come up with a toilet seat with a built in bidet mechanism. The seat is ergonomically designed with soft curves, a low front, and a high back. I don't know about the rest of you, but I don't think I'd be all that comfortable on a toilet seat that had me leaning forward all of the time. It would greatly reduce the enjoyment of the interlude if I had to be in constant fear of sliding off the seat.

What really strikes fear into my heart is the optional heater. I really don't think I would be comfortable sitting down on a toilet seat that is plugged into the wall socket. Somehow I think the combination of a tank full of water and electricity flowing through the seat is just a little too close to the concept of an electric chair. I could see myself uncomfortably seated on its ergonomic design, reading a magazine, hoping I could maintain my balance on the slope, and accidentally hitting the wrong button on the seat's remote control. In my haste to escape the water aimed at those sensitive regions, I could quite possibly damage the device, causing a short circuit in the wiring. I'd be reduced to a bowlful of ashes.

. . . albeit a gently showered and cleansed bowlful of ashes, ready for immediate burial at sea.

Hospitals can be hazardous to your health.

The government should force every hospital to put that statement in bold letters on every entrance to their building. After all, people die there. While I cannot personally claim to have died in a hospital, I can attest to several incidents that left me either sure I was about to or wishing I would.

A number of years ago I sustained a severe spinal injury in a serious golfing accident. No, I didn't belong to an Australian Rules, Full Contact Golf and Country Club. My car was rear-ended while I was on the way to the golf course. This event had a fairly major impact on my handicap. Two years later, I was rear-ended by a driver suffering the effects of a nasty hangover. Two years after that, an RCMP officer drove his 4-wheel drive multi-passenger utility vehicle into the back of my van. He said he hit me because anti-lock brakes don't work well on dry pavement.

Like maybe that was my fault . . . ?

Since that time I have been tested, injected, CT Scanned, MRI'ed, Bone Scanned, and have undergone just about every procedure known to inquisitive physicians.

The myleogram stands out as the event that brought me closest to having a death wish while wearing a hospital gown. Whoever came up with this little gem must have been particularly sadistic.

I could almost picture Dr. Frank N. Stein turning to his surgical resident and saying, "I've got it. We'll suck out his spinal fluid, replace it with a radioactive mixture, and watch it slosh around inside him on an X-ray machine. We'll turn him this way and that way, and we'll even tip him upside down. Even if his head doesn't explode when the radioactivity gets to his brain, just watching his facial expression will be worth the price of admission."

The bone scan is another gem. They strap you to a table, inject a little radioactive fluid leftover from the myleogram, and take a couple of gazillion X-rays. It is somewhat disconcerting to be lying there wearing nothing but a bit of pale blue cotton that doesn't even cover what you really want to have covered, and suddenly notice that everyone else in the room is wearing enough lead to withstand a nuclear holocaust.

One of the tests that doctors like to put spine-injured patients through is called an evoked potentials test. You might recall applying electricity to dead frogs in high school biology class. The concept is the same except I get to play the role of the frog. Some states have decided that electrocution is cruel and unusual punishment for mass-murderers, but they still let doctors order an evoked potentials test on innocent newspaper columnists.

I recently let my doctor talk me into having another evoked potentials test. ("You never know. It might tell us something new . . . ") In my mind, I could hear myself screaming emphatically that there was no way I was going to go through that again. Unfortunately, my mouth wasn't paying attention to my mind and it said, "Oh, Okay I guess . . . "

Some of the nerves to my lower extremities are still functioning, leaving me with approximately 65 percent use of my right leg and 20 percent of my left. While the other nerves couldn't feel the electricity, the working ones most definitely could. The technician seemed to enjoy finding those working nerves. He cranked up the juice until I said I could feel it. Then he cranked it up even more. Parts of my body that hadn't moved in years were doing the Macarena. I knew I was going to have to dig up my little bottle of super-deluxe, extra-strength, mind-numbing painkillers when I got home.

That's when the trouble really started.

The painkillers put me into a blissful state of semi-consciousness. I knew everything still hurt, but I just didn't give a damn. Eventually I fell asleep, only to be awakened by my wife and sons returning from the grocery store. I completely forgot about being spine-injured. I stood up from the bed, and missed. The floor wasn't damaged, but I broke three ribs, necessitating another round of super-deluxe, extra-strength, mind-numbing painkillers.

Magnetic Resonance Imaging is another non-favorite of mine. Dr. Curious George ordered one of those at the same time as he thought of the evoked potentials test. He pointed out that, for some reason, the previous time I had undergone this test they hadn't scanned my spine.

"They only looked at your head, so obviously they didn't find anything," he said.

I wasn't sure whether I should be insulted or take it as a good reason to go back inside the tube, lovingly referred to as Claustrophobic's Nightmare.

Whoever designed the MRI machine never had to get inside it. It's a long tube, with a diameter barely big enough to accommodate the average human body. Therein lies the problem. I do not have the average human body. I just barely fit in the thing five years ago. I assumed that it would be easier this time because I have lost about sixty pounds in the interim.

I assumed wrong.

I guess I should be proud of the fact that I have added several inches of muscle mass to my upper body as a result of maneuvering around on forearm crutches and in a wheelchair. Unfortunately, the extra dimensions made me too big for the MRI.

After failing at her first attempt to ram me head first into the machine, the technician was undaunted. She decided to try cramming me in, with one arm raised over my head, a position I wasn't too anxious to hold for the next two hours. Again, I was wedged in the entrance.

Her next idea was even less appealing. She decided to raise both my arms, and give the table another mighty push into the opening.

The bruises are healing nicely thank you.

"Perhaps if we amputate your arms . . . " she mused out loud.

"Test over!" I cried. "I drove myself here and I need something to hold onto the steering wheel with, on the way home."

The next doctor who wants me to undergo some new test to get a better look at the parts of me that don't do what they are supposed to anymore had better be willing to get into the machine himself first.

If he won't, I won't.

You Call That A Prank . . . Now Here's A Real Prank

You'd think I was living in Chechnya, Lebanon, or South Central Los Angeles. Another missile attack hit my house last night. I'm not sure what terrorist organization is responsible for these attacks, but I don't think they are particularly well funded. Their weapons of choice are limited to manually-launched, ground-to-window eggs.

I can't tell you how thoroughly I enjoy starting the day by hosing down the front of my house. If you've never had the experience, let me tell you that egg, when scrambled raw on a window, quickly dries to the consistency of igneous rock.

While I don't know the proper names of the individuals who perpetrated this guerilla attack, I do have several preferred ways of referring to them — none of which can be printed in a mainstream newspaper. Let's just say that I generally make an inference about the marital status of their parents, the canine lineage on their maternal side, and the lack of intelligence in their rectums.

Frankly, I have to feel a bit sorry for anyone who cannot come up with a more original prank. Egging a house doesn't take much in the way of planning. I, on the other hand, have been involved in some absolutely glorious pranks — practical jokes that even left the recipients saying, "Wow! That really took a lot of thought to come up with an idea like that. Now come here so I can hit you."

Take, for example, the great heavyweight telephone bout of 1976. That was a prank that really should go down in history. At the time I worked in an office of the federal government. Oh, Okay, I was employed by the federal government; working was not a real requirement of the job. That left us with lots of time on our hands to develop highly detailed attacks on our co-workers.

There was one of those guys there; the sort you find in every office. He thought he was one of the great examples of athletic prowess and felt that everyone should be aware of his abilities in any and every sport. Logically, he was the perfect target for the great heavyweight telephone bout.

In those days, telephone receivers could be easily taken apart. The mouthpiece and the earpiece simply unscrewed from the handle. The handle was hollow, except for a couple of thin wires. As a result it was the perfect storage place for things you didn't want others to know about. In this case we started storing small lead weights in the target's telephone receiver. We put cotton balls in there to keep the weights from moving around and exposing the prank before it could reach its spectacular conclusion.

Each day his telephone became a bit heavier. At first it was barely noticeable. After a couple of weeks, he started to rub his bicep whenever he answered the phone. By the time we filled the receiver handle to capacity, it weighed over two pounds, and he was convinced that he had somehow injured his arm because the receiver seemed so heavy. He even complained to others in the office that he must have torn a muscle while pitching, but that it only seemed to bother him when he had to pick up the phone.

Unbeknownst to him, everyone in the office, from the kid in the mailroom to the head of the department was in on what was going on with his phone. We would all take any opportunity to borrow his phone. When we did, we'd lift the receiver as though nothing was amiss.

We left the telephone at its full weight for nearly two weeks and arranged for him to receive lots of 'wrong number' calls from friends in other offices so he would become used to the excess weight. Then, one Monday morning, we all arrived at work early enough to remove the lead from his telephone before he arrived and to witness the culmination of over a month's worth of plotting. As soon as he sat down, we called his extension. He lifted the receiver with the amount of force he had become used to using. The result was spectacular. The much lighter telephone receiver collided with the side of his head making a sound that reminded us all of that noise you hear when you knock on an overripe watermelon.

So these window eggers had better be forewarned. If I am ever able to identify them, I might just come up with a really creative way to retaliate. I'm thinking along the lines of an automatic sprinkler system that is controlled by the sound of an egg hitting the window. Perhaps I could fill the sprinkler heads with purple material dye.

. . . or maybe . . . no that would be too cruel. Let me get back to you when I've thought it all through . . .

North Carolina, (why does it always have to be someplace like North Carolina?) has recently passed a law that prohibits the transport of a dead body in the passenger seat of a car.

Ever since that little bit of news crossed my desk, I've been trying to come up with a reason that might make me want to transport a dead body in the passenger seat of my car. I hate to disappoint you but I actually came up with a couple of fairly good reasons.

For example, you could be tired of watching other drivers zip along the car-pool lanes on the freeway, while you sit alone in your car in the slow lane behind an octogenarian in a motor home who is talking on his cellular phone while trying to warm up a cup of coffee in his microwave. The addition of a cadaver in the passenger seat would give you the appearance of driving for a car pool, and speed your rush hour drives.

A dead body in the passenger seat might actually be better than some of the car pools I've ridden in over the years. For one thing, it is bound to smell better. Odds are that the level of conversation could reach a substantially higher intellectual plane, too.

Not satisfied to relegate the transportation of the dearly departed to the back seat, or perhaps the trunk, the North Carolina state legislators decided that the delicate sensitivities of dead bodies should also be protected. The law went on to ban the use of "indecent or obscene language in the presence of a dead body."

Talk about spoilsports.

What fun is a funeral without a few good jokes; especially the kind that make use of indecent or obscene language and preferably at the expense of the deceased. The occasional, well-timed bit of indecent language, depending on the definition of indecent, can be quite useful in trying to make someone else at the funeral laugh.

The whole thing was at the behest of the North Carolina Board of Mortuary Science. That, of course, translates into the undertakers' association. They don't like the word undertaker anymore. Ever since the garbagemen became sanitary engineers, anyone with a less than tasteful job title has been looking for a happier sounding name for their profession.

I don't think the lawmakers thought through all the potential consequences of their decision before enacting the bill. It didn't take me too long before I was able to come up with a perfectly legitimate case for the use of profanity in front of a dead body.

Put yourself in this situation. You're out walking your dog at night. Perhaps it's a dark and stormy night. As you wander along the paths waiting for the dog to remember why the two of you have gone out, you trip over a person who has neglected to breathe for a considerable period of time.

Somehow I don't think you are going to say, "Gosh! I've tripped over a dead body."

I'd find it equally implausible to suspect that you might say, "Well, I'll be darned. I wonder who left this formerly living person right here where I could trip over him."

Let's face it. You're going to let loose a string of words that can't be published in a mainstream newspaper, aren't you?

I know I would.

Even those very same undertakers who want to be called practitioners of mortuary science might have cause to let loose with the occasional four-letter explicative in the presence of a person who no longer keeps a rhythm with his heartbeat. Take, for instance, the people at the funeral home that cremated the wrong body a few months ago. I'm sure when they saw what they had done, they didn't say things like "Gee willackers" or "Gosh-golly. I didn't mean to do that."

When my time comes, and I certainly hope it isn't for a good long while, I don't think I'd mind if you propped me up in the passenger seat of the car and took me for a drive. If you felt the need you could probably also point out that I looked like a piece of . . . well . . . you know the word.

Just be forewarned. If you do decide to take me for a posthumous trip, let's not go to North Carolina. I don't want to end up in jail in this life or the next.

How Can I Make A Comeback When I Don't Have An 'Already Done That'?

Boy, I've made some mistakes in my time. If I could I'd kick myself over this latest one. They say that those who fail to plan, plan to fail, and I really should have planned things out a whole lot better than I did.

The fact that I am only now recognizing the huge tactical error I made years ago will do nothing for me. I only hope that admitting it publicly will prevent some of our younger generation from making the same mistakes I did. Perhaps my sons will learn from my bad example and act now to prevent them from realizing that they are in the same boat when it's their turn to have fifty looming on the horizon.

Had I known then what has become so painfully obvious to me this week I might have been better prepared. Who knew that economies would change so much? If I had just organized my life a bit better I might have had some type of career that I could return to for over a million dollars a year.

Mario Lemieux did it last year when he returned to the ice for the Pittsburgh Penguins. Now Michael Jordan is coming back to basketball. Why didn't I think of something like that?

Okay, I guess it might have something to do with the fact that I'm not an athlete. Maybe if I had planned it better I could have been one, but then again I have certain limitations that would keep me from most of the good paying sports jobs. I'm 6' 4". That's maybe a bit short for the NBA, and I wouldn't want to be seen dribbling in public, so I guess basketball is out. It's probably a bit too tall for hockey, besides, I've never been able to find a pair of skates that I could put on the bottoms of my crutches, and they don't leave me any free hands to hold the hockey stick. Football is out. I'm not a big fan of having guys the size of dump trucks jumping on top of me. A genetic disorder prevents me from playing baseball. I have what is referred to in the medical texts as ball-strike narcolepsy. It causes me to fall asleep if I try to watch baseball — usually somewhere around the midpoint of the top of the first inning.

Of course, there is always acting. In my youth I had a very promising career on the stage. Maybe some producer out there might want to pay me buckets full of money to reprise my high school starring roles as Third Guy From The Left in the chorus of *Annie Get Your Gun* or Man At The First Desk in *How To Succeed In Business Without Really Trying*. I don't think the world is ready to see me, at my current state of girth, wearing a toga, so you probably won't want to see me redo my brilliant interpretation of the role of Assassin Number Three in *Julius Caesar*.

Singing is definitely out. Even when I was the aforementioned Third Guy From The Left in the chorus of *Annie Get Your Gun*, the director preferred that I lip-synched the words and let the rest of the chorus carry the tune, something he suggested I might have trouble doing with a front-end loader. Of course that doesn't seem to be stopping so many of the acts on the current concert tours. Apparently they would sound too out of breath if they tried to sing and dance at the same time, so people are paying a hundred dollars to listen to the artists' compact disk while they just dance around the stage.

Art might be a possibility. My son is taking an art appreciation course and he tells me that the professor said that if someone threw a coffee cup onto a pile of rocks, swept up the mess, and displayed it in a gallery, no one has the right to say that it isn't "art." I wonder what I could get for the artistic rendering I created this morning when I accidentally kicked over the cat's litter box.

There is one way I could get a million or two based on my previous education and experience. Obviously Michael Jordan was lucky enough to have a gym teacher who took the time to extol the benefits of a properly executed free throw. I think I'll sue my old high school for wasting my time with all that history, English, and math. Their negligence has certainly deprived me of the opportunity to make a million-dollar comeback in my forties.

It's either that or keep praying for a lotto windfall . . .

I'm all for protecting endangered species. One of the highlights of my working life was being a student teacher at a science school in the mid-Seventies. Part of my duties was to introduce students, some as young as kindergarten, to an arctic wolf that had been rescued as an orphaned pup. I quickly developed a special bond with that animal and even now, over twenty-five years later, I can still see him in my mind's eye like it was yesterday.

I am not a hunter. Not that I don't believe there is a place in the ecosystem for hunters, I'm just not sure of the wisdom of letting someone like me fire a gun.

I am opposed to the slaughter of animals just to harvest various body parts for their supposed aphrodisiac properties. If you want a bear's gall bladder, you should give the bear an equal chance. Forget the rifles. If you can get its gall bladder before it gets yours, then you can keep it, otherwise the bear wins.

That said, I'm still a bit bewildered over the extent to which some people will go to increase the world's population of various species. One such case came to light this week.

We all know that pandas are one of the most endangered species. The big problem, according to Chinese state media, isn't from an inability to mate, but from a fundamental lack of interest in sex. Apparently, new techniques are being used to heighten panda bears' libidos. Chinese panda authorities are excited about the results of their new program. Already thirteen pandas are pregnant, half of them with twins. This jump in pregnancies has been attributed to a unique tool they've put into use over there.

Panda Porn . . .

Last year the authorities in Sichuan started showing the pandas movies of other pandas mating in an attempt to arouse the males. The mind reels at the thought. Okay, maybe yours doesn't, but mine sure does.

Do these movies feature well-endowed female pandas cavorting through bamboo groves with little or no clothes, plot, or dialogue? Do the female pandas put on seductive negligees and wait by the door hoping to seduce muscular bamboo delivery boys? I can just imagine the titles: Lusty Ling-Ling, Ping-Ping Does Peking, or perhaps, Quing-Quang Quickies. I think I saw that last one late at night on the Discovery Channel.

It seems they are also offering the younger pandas a sex education program that involves letting them watch their elders mate. They think that will arouse their interest.

I'm not sure about the validity of that concept. Quick, picture your parents having sex. Now think about it. Didn't that seem to have the reverse effect?

My wife and I could reduce our sons to quivering by saying anything that remotely gave the indication that their parents would do that sort of thing. In order to get the image out of his mind, our oldest would cover his ears and say "pink flamingoes" over and over, in the hope that he could replace the vile images running through his mind with a scene of flamingoes wading in a tropical pool.

Because watching them quiver was so much fun we used to say things like, "Say dear, how about a little pink flamingo after dinner," just to watch his reaction. The image never did much for me. I don't think I could do much of anything if I had to stand on one leg in a foot of water while I was doing it.

Reports that the Chinese scientists were giving the male pandas Viagra™ were denied. That story resulted from a Chinese reporter misunderstanding a joke. "Did you hear the one about the panda on Viagra™ . . . ?" They did admit to testing some traditional herbal aphrodisiacs, but said they just made the males aggressive with their mates. I wonder if that meant the pandas wanted to wear leather thongs and experiment with that whole bondage and whips thing.

I think the credit for the success is really attributable to one small aspect of the program. The panda authorities came up with a brilliant idea. Instead of keeping the animals cooped up alone all the time they started letting the males and females socialize and play together. What a concept! Who would have thought that giving the animals a chance to hang out together, share a bit of bamboo, and take a romantic walk in the grove might get them in the mood to go back to his place, watch a little panda porn, and slip into something more comfortable?

It will be easy to spot the ones too young to mate. They'll be the ones with their paws over their eyes trying to picture pink flamingoes.

All along I knew it had to be good for something. Now here I am sitting on "a potential treasure." All those people who told me I should do something about it are going to be sorry now.

I sat down to read the newspaper the other day and I could hardly believe my eyes. The headline, right on the front page, gave my self-worth an incredible burst. What was once thought of as a shortcoming would now and forever be a source of great pride, and potential wealth.

"Unwanted Human Fat A Potential Treasure."

Be still my heart. I finally have a reason to be thankful that I have never been able to lose the weight my wife gained during pregnancy.

If there is one thing that I have an oversupply of, it's unwanted human fat. I'm sitting on a whole pile of it right now. I have another store of it where one might expect my lap to be, if it wasn't hidden by my potential treasure trove of a gut.

It looks like, American scientists have discovered a way to harvest stem cells from human fat. I think I have a lot of stem cells. A Douglas fir with a stem as big around as I am would be somewhere in the neighborhood of seventy-five feet tall.

The stem cells they are talking about are human cells that can be reprogrammed to produce muscle, bone, or cartilage, as well as possibly being the building blocks from which new organs could be grown to replace damaged or diseased ones. Before this recent discovery, stem cells were harvested from bone marrow, brain, and fetal tissue. As a result, there was a shortage of supply and various groups felt that there were ethical issues that should preclude using stem cells from some sources.

Fat doesn't have ethical issues, just aesthetic ones.

It's an incredible breakthrough for medical science. Just think, some day part of my fatty treasure chest could be used to grow a new ear for any boxer foolish enough to step into the ring with Mike Tyson. My spare tire could probably grow enough new cartilage for the knees of every player in the National Football League, the National Hockey League, and still have some left over for Tonya Harding's figure skating opponents.

Just think of the linguistic changes that could occur thanks to this discovery. The politically correct language police could have a heyday. No longer will people be subjected to terms like fat, chubby, pudgy, chunky, lardbutt, or thunder-thighs. Skinny people (the stem cell disenfranchised) will be forced to refer to us as stem cell enhanced or stem cell endowed.

This might even give those of us who are in possession of excessive reserves of stem cells a chance to get back at all those thin people who have acted so superior over the years. We could create our own stem cell cartel, and demand ever-increasing prices for our natural resources. It's worked well for the OPEC countries, so it should work for us, too. There should be an automatic tripling of our stem cell prices for those people who can eat ice cream, chocolate bars, pie, and donuts without gaining any weight.

Apparently, the new tissues created from stem cells will have a greatly reduced chance of being rejected. Now that's poetic justice isn't it? All the fat people who were ever rejected for dates by skinny people could one day be providing those same stem cell disadvantaged people with rejection-proof organs.

There could be long-term income potential here. I could sit on this nest egg or liquidate my fat reserves as the need for extra income arises. If I get short of cash I could just go out and eat a couple gallons of Ben and Jerry's finest, wash it down with two or three-dozen beer, and wend my way down to the stem cell bank to make a deposit.

I could probably have my own gross national product.

Marc Hedrick of the University of California at Los Angeles led the study that made this discovery. With all the liposuction that goes on in Los Angeles, I'm sure they had no shortage of stem cells for their research. I just hope that all those Californians aren't going to flood the market and reduce the value of my flank account.

I had always hoped that one day I'd have a nice fat wallet. I assumed that if I ever did, it would be filled with money. My wallet has gotten so fat it barely fits in my pants pocket, but it isn't money that has caused my billfold bulge. It's plastic cards — over forty of them. If a pickpocket ever tried to slip it out of my pocket, he wouldn't get much money, and he'd probably get a hernia for his efforts.

If I didn't know better, I'd say that they were multiplying through some sort of asexual reproduction.

I'm almost certain that the day I leave one of them in my desk drawer will be the day I actually need it. When I look at some of them, it takes me a while to remember what purpose they serve, but I am convinced that someday they'll be useful, even if it's just scraping frost from my car's windshield.

Sure, some of them are important. Obviously, I need to carry my driver's license. Without it, how would anyone know I've said they can use whatever internal parts of me can be recycled through an organ donor program? I just hope that they make very sure that I'm actually finished with them before they rip out my heart, lungs, liver, kidneys, or nasal passages. Can you imagine waking up from a coma, only to find your heart beating in someone else's chest?

I have four grocery store identification cards, one pet store card, an office supply store card, a bookstore card, and one from a drugstore. These aren't credit cards, they are the ones stores have been giving out to keep track of how many tubes of toothpaste, tons of kitty litter, and notepaper pads people buy. Only two of them have my name printed on them, and just one has my photograph. Well, at least I think it's my photograph. The picture is so incredibly out of focus it looks like I'm having an out-of-body experience.

Four cards are for airline mileage plans. I'm sure if you combined all of the miles I've accumulated among them, I might qualify for an economy class ticket from Sault Ste. Marie, Ontario, across the river to Sault Ste. Marie, Michigan, should I ever have the desire to visit either of those two cities.

There are six prepaid telephone long distance cards taking up space in my wallet. Most of them only have a little bit of time left, but you never know when I might be on the road and decide that I want to pick up a telephone in Nashville and talk to my brother in Toronto for eleven seconds.

I have three automated teller machine cards. Two of them are for my bank in Canada, and one for the one I use in the United States. It's reassuring to know that I can pull up to a drive-through bank machine at any hour of the day or night and check to see how far overdrawn all my bank accounts are.

Aside from the two Visa cards I carry, there are an additional three store and one gas station credit card adding to the plastic menagerie. Most people might find it hard to believe that, despite my professed lack of handyman skills, I actually carry a Home Depot credit card.

It sure came in handy last week when I bought my wife a new toilet seat for Valentine's Day. She didn't seem to get the significance that it was kind of heart shaped.

Now I'm waiting for someone handy to come along and install it for me.

I'm not sure what was wrong with the old one, but Diane kept complaining that it was never in the correct position when she went to use it, so I can only assume it must have been malfunctioning somehow. It always seemed to be in the proper, up, position when either of the boys or I needed to use it.

I have a plastic card from an airline that says I'm insured if I'm ever in a plane crash. I suppose it's reassuring that the airline doesn't expect it to be one of the first things to melt when the jet fuel explodes on impact. There are three or four other insurance cards in there that should convince worried emergency room staff I'm insured for the heart attack they are ignoring.

The rest of the wallet contains membership cards, video rental cards, and even a prepaid card for the photocopiers at the library.

It's probably just as well that I don't have much money. There wouldn't be room for it in my wallet.

It was HOW long ago?

I suffered through another wave of nostalgia, when the thirtieth anniversary of Neil Armstrong's giant step, crept up on me unexpectedly. How could it be over thirty years ago? Mathematically adding thirty to the age I was at the time did equal my age at the time, but philosophically, I'm not a day more than ten years older. I don't want to accept that thirty years has past, but the world seems to be force-feeding me the facts. If one more person had asked me where I was when I first heard "That's one small step for man, one giant leap for mankind," I might have been inclined to send them into a geo-synchronous orbit.

I suppose it's one of those milepost events in our collective consciousness. People who witness momentous occasions, even if only through the media, tend to remember the minute details surrounding those frozen moments in time. For some strange reason, though, we seem addicted to sharing and re-sharing those moments again and again. I'm just glad our memories can filter out the more meaningless events in our lives. It's one thing to remember where you were when Armstrong walked on the moon, but I'd hate to imagine what the world would be like if people started asking each other where they were when they heard the news that Wilma Flintstone was expecting Bam-Bam.

I suppose a thirtieth anniversary of an event like walking on the moon is something that we should take note of as it passes. I prefer to remember the little stranger elements to these events. For example, ever since Armstrong made that momentous descent down the ladder into the soft dust of the Sea of Tranquility, there have been rumors floating around that he sidestepped Buzz Aldrin to get to the door first. I've always secretly believed that the two of them played a deep space version of odds and evens to make the final decision about who got first dibs on the seat by the door.

Another amusing lunar landing story is currently traveling through cyberspace. It concerns Armstrong's comments after he finished bouncing around on the moon's surface as if it was some kind of trampoline. He is reported to have said, "Good luck, Mr. Gorsky," before reentering the lunar landing vehicle. If you believe the tale, he has just recently come clean about what the comment supposedly meant. Apparently, when he was a small boy, he overheard his neighbors, the Gorskys, arguing. Mrs. Gorsky is reported to have said, "Sex? . . . Sex? . . . I'll tell you when you'll have sex . . . when the kid next door walks on the moon!" I'd love to believe that it's true, but I've listened to copies of the transmissions from the moon on a CD-ROM I bought a few years ago. Sadly, I heard no mention of Mr. Gorsky.

There is still a chance that the story is true. Remember that Armstrong's Commander-In-Chief in those days was Richard Nixon, and he was always having trouble with bits of tape being erased.

Okay, I'll admit that the lunar landing impressed me when it happened, but a few weeks later I was even more impressed with an event that held greater significance for teenagers in the Sixties:

Woodstock.

Frankly, it scares the heck out of me to realize that since July 1999 marked the thirtieth anniversary of Apollo 11's trip to the moon and back, August 1999 marked the thirtieth anniversary of hundreds of thousands of trips to, and a great many trips of another kind in, Upstate New York. Just a couple weeks after Neil Armstrong's immortal words rang around the world, Max Yazgur uttered his phrase, "I'm just a farmer . . . " to a massive crowd of rain drenched hippies.

It seems almost like a desecration of our collective memories to see scenes of Woodstock being used to sell a feminine hygiene product on television today. Maybe it's just a guy thing. We don't like thinking about those products at the best of times, but to stimulate our memories of the Woodstock era for twenty-five seconds, only to dash them by mentioning a product of that particular nature . . . well, it's just wrong, wrong, wrong.

Those of you who recall the Sixties, even if your memory is sketchy, or pock-marked and pot-holed with drug-induced lapses, should remember that, at the time, we were all being told not to trust anyone over the age of thirty. It pains me to realize that the four babies who were born during the concert at Woodstock have turned thirty themselves. It makes me wonder:

Who are they going to trust?

I admit I'm not overly computer literate. I can't get too excited about the latest bells and whistles that seem to enthrall so many other people. I only use my computer for writing my column, doing research on the Internet, and handling my e-mail. I know what e-mail I want to send. I also have a pretty good idea about what e-mail I want to receive. I can control the former, but the latter seems to have gotten completely and utterly out of control.

I receive between 75 and 125 e-mails each day. Many of them I delete as soon as they come in. These are the ones from people who are living under a false impression that I might be interested in getting involved in a multi-level marketing scheme, continuing the seemingly immortal life of yet another chain letter, or reading the same joke for the 400th time this month.

For some reason, I seem to get several e-mails each week that are copies of the *You Might Be A Redneck If . . .* comedy monologues by Jeff Foxworthy. The originator of these e-mails never gives Foxworthy credit for the material, even though anyone who has ever listened to one of his recorded appearances or read one of his books can quickly identify the source. As someone who enjoys this particular comedian, I've heard or read them all. I don't need to get any unsolicited plagiarism of his copyright protected work appearing in my e-mail box every couple of days.

I should have died a thousand deaths by now for not forwarding chain letters to ten, twenty, or fifty of my closest personal friends. If I had forwarded all of the chain letters I receive each month, I can assure you that I probably would have lost my ten, twenty, or fifty closest friends by now. Usually I don't even know the person who forwards the things to me in the first place, but obviously they consider me one of their close personal friends.

Some chain letters follow the standard format. If you forward them you will receive good luck, thousands of dollars, and a long and happy life. They contain references to people who have broken the chain and within days have fallen under the wheels of a bus, or been bitten by venomous fish that suddenly and inexplicably inhabited their swimming pool. Others are more geared to the people who have no idea how e-mail works. One of these new cyberspace chain letters suggests that some computerized form of Big Brother will know whenever someone forwards it to someone else. According to the letter, everyone who forwards it will get a free trip to Disney World. The letter says that Bill Gates and Walt Disney's son sponsor this promotion. Frankly, I think Bill Gates has better things to do, and I have to wonder how Walt Disney came to have a son when his wife bore only daughters.

I've decided that I will start replying to all of these e-mail messages with a form letter you might want to use if you are being similarly flooded with cyber junk mail.

Dear Sir Madam:

You have been selected to receive this fascinating e-mail because you somehow managed to select me to receive your chain letter, pyramid marketing scheme, or the 346th copy of the joke about the old lady who is sorry she neutered her cat when her fairy godmother turned him into a handsome prince.

In addition, by opening this e-mail message you have unleashed the mother of all computer viruses. Within the next few minutes it will do the following:

•Determine your credit card number and its available balance. It will then use it to open subscriptions to every available pornographic Internet service until your card is maxed out.

•Forward letters to your spouse, your church, your employer, your former Scout leader, and your mother listing the pornographic web pages you subscribe to.

•Put your name on the mailing list of every chain letter and multilevel sales scam.

•Cause your computer to emit hypersonic waves that will tie-dye all of your dress clothes, attract an infestation of crickets into your bedroom, spay or neuter your neighbor's dog, cause the eggs in your refrigerator to explode (but only if you pick them up and are dressed and running late for work), and infect you with a serious case of nasal congestion, athlete's foot, and gingivitis.

I doubt if this letter will deter any of the perpetrators of the junk e-mail that is constantly filling up my Internet mailbox, but at least it will waste a bit of their time dealing with my response.

And that has to be worth something.

Perhaps it's the weather. It might be the after effect of those Indian nuclear tests. Whatever it is, I wish it would stop putting me so close to people who insist on being dumber than a sack of rusty hammers. Some of the people I've come across in the last couple of weeks make my dog look like a candidate for Mensa.

I try to avoid spending much time around courthouses, but the other day I accompanied my oldest son when he had to testify in a case. Something told me the defendants weren't the smartest people on Earth. They had broken into the store where Mike works while it was still open.

Mike was scheduled to testify at 10:00 AM. We arrived on time, despite having one of those days when every traffic signal turns red just as we approached it, the drivers ahead of me insisted on cruising down the passing lane at fifteen miles per hour below the posted limit, and every route we picked was slowed by road construction.

The clerk directed us to a waiting room where we did just as the sign directed. We waited, and we waited . . . and waited . . . and waited . . .

Finally, after an hour the prosecutor came out to speak to Mike. One of the defendants had pled guilty. The other one was having difficulty making up his mind whether he was guilty or not.

So we waited . . . and waited . . . and waited some more.

Eventually, Mike was called into the courtroom to testify. The indecisive member of this criminal brain trust sat alone at the defense table. He had decided to plead not guilty and to represent himself in the case. There is a saying about people who represent themselves having fools for clients. If ever there was a need to prove the validity of that statement, it could certainly be found in this case.

The prosecutor asked Mike a few general questions about the layout of his place of employment, and how he and his boss came upon the gang who couldn't think straight trying to remove merchandise from the storeroom. He then asked about the clothes the men were wearing.

"One of them had on a suit," said Mike.

"What colour was it?" asked the attorney.

"It was over a year ago, and I only saw him for a moment, but I think it was green," answered Mike.

With that, the guy who couldn't decide whether or not he was guilty of breaking into a store while it was still open looked up and Mike and nodded, as though to say, "Yeah, you're right, Man. It was green."

That's when I realized I was sitting behind the defendant's parents. The man turned to his wife and said, "The boy definitely got his brains from your side of the family. This proves he's almost as stupid as your brother."

I wish I could say that that has been my only experience with sheer stupidity in the last couple of weeks. I found someone almost as bright when I tried crossing into the United States on the Saturday of the

Victoria Day weekend, a long weekend in Canada a week before Memorial Day.

I reached the border lineup at 7:00 AM. I made it to the border, about a quarter of a mile further, at ten after eight. There was only one checkpoint open, and the woman wanted to check everyone's trunk.

When I finally got to the front of the line, she looked in my window and asked, "Do you have any drugs or weapons on board?"

"Well, no Ma'am, I don't," I said, just before hearing one of the stupidest questions ever.

"But tell me," I heard my own voice saying, "does anyone ever say yes?"

I knew right away that it was probably the stupidest thing I had ever said. The exhaust fumes I'd been inhaling for the previous hour and ten minutes had probably killed a few million brain cells. At least, that's the excuse I'm sticking with.

The stupidity of the question obviously surprised the customs officer, too. She gave me one of those looks that told me I might soon be learning the true meaning of the term 'government probe'.

Luckily for me, she decided that if I was stupid enough to ask a question like that, I probably wouldn't be smart enough to hide drugs or weapons on my body. She restricted her search of my nooks and crannies to the ones that were part of the car. My personal nooks and crannies were left unprobed.

It just goes to show that in a momentary lapse, anyone can say or do something that raises the level of world stupidity a bit.

I guess I shouldn't be so hard on my dog.

Unlike my sons, I am not a huge fan of computer games.

For that matter, I'm not even that big a fan of computers. Don't get me wrong, I'm not anti-computer either. I just don't look at them the same way some people do. For me, my computer is just a tool I use to get my job done. Since I'm not overly handy with any other kinds of tools, power or otherwise, I don't attempt to do anything too fancy with my computer. As long as it has enough power to get my column out each week, keep track of where I'm supposed to be, when and with whom, I'm generally satisfied.

Earlier this year my computer satisfaction was at an all time low, as it refused to do anything I asked it to do. Even when my computer is functioning normally, it refuses to do what I want it to do if I attempt to play most computer games.

Brad has quite a collection of computer games based on the *Star Wars* phenomenon. The Force is not with me in any of those games. I cannot pilot an X-Wing. I couldn't hit the side of a barn with a laser-enhanced ion cannon if my life depended on it. Truth be known, I'm usually quite dead before I get my spacecraft out of the hanger. As a result, I avoid *Star Wars* games.

I'm no better at ridding the world of evil, time-traveling robots. Even though I seem to be armed with more weapons of mass destruction than existed prior to 1998, I am totally useless as a defender of life, liberty and justice. Within seconds, the robot hordes come out of nowhere and eliminate all of the Earth's flora, fauna, and the bacterial culture needed to produce frozen yogurt.

I was never much good with real guns, and perhaps it's the memory of my few shooting experiences that haunt me whenever I try to fire a bazooka on the computer. The first time I ever fired a shotgun was a memorable event. No one bothered to tell me to hold the butt of the gun tightly against my shoulder. They also didn't mention that you are only supposed to pull one trigger at a time. Those of you who are used to firing shotguns will have already pictured the result. When the two shells erupted from the chambers, I was immediately propelled backwards with what was left of my right shoulder leading the way by an extra foot or two.

I even tried shooting a gun from my wheelchair once. I was in the desert outside Phoenix, Arizona. I was given the chance to fire a .45 Magnum handgun at some beer cans planted into the side of a cliff. I had seen Clint Eastwood fire a .45 Magnum as though it was a cap gun, so I assumed it was a pretty easy thing to do. Firing the gun was, in fact, quite easy. Recovering from the jolt was something else all together. When I pulled the trigger, the ensuing recoil moved the chair back nearly three feet in the soft sand. I'm sure that if I hadn't set the brakes before firing the gun it would have pushed me all the way back to Phoenix.

My lack of prowess with guns, real or imaginary, has never really bothered me too much. My lack of skill at computer games does seem to be a source of concern for my sons. When I try to get a space ship out of the hangar without killing myself and all the other life forms on the mother ship, my sons speak to me in the same sort of tones that my father used when I tried to use a hand tool. I have almost as good an aim with a hammer as I do with a photon array on the computer. It's probably safest for all concerned if I stay away from either one.

My sons don't seem to believe that it is possible to function without some sort of computer enhanced entertainment. Obviously concerned for my mental well-being, Brad gave me a computer game for Christmas last year. Most of the programs on the disk produce card games that seem to fit Brad's image of my computer game playing capability. I'm actually doing pretty well on a couple of them. One game in particular keeps track of my winnings in dollar amounts. Right now, my computer owes me $2,502.

If I could just figure out how to collect what it owes me, I'd buy a computer that would let me win the other games, too.

Traveling Down The Road Of Life
Without A Map Or Directions

"CAUTION HORSES"

We've all seen those words painted on the back of horse trailers. Until last week I thought they were rather redundant. What else is going to be riding in a horse trailer?

Let's face it. It's not very likely that the horses are going to open the trailer door and attack another motorist, so the only real purpose of the words 'Caution Horses' is to advise everyone that the driver of the vehicle pulling the trailer has some expensive horseflesh loaded in the trailer.

At least that's what I thought until last week.

I was driving home in heavy traffic on Interstate 5 through Washington. All four northbound lanes of the highway were filled with commuters wishing they were somewhere else and frustrated by the traffic that was preventing them from getting there. Instead of the posted seventy miles per hour, traffic coasted along at about forty. Adding to everyone's frustration was an excessive summer temperature that seemed to overtax the capabilities of everyone's air conditioning.

Just ahead, and one lane to my right, was a pick-up truck towing a horse trailer. The top half of the back doors of the trailer had been left open to allow the animal to enjoy a bit of fresh air. It was a very pretty gray mare.

She had a jet-black tail that she'd somehow managed to flip over the tailgate so that it blew back and forth in the breeze as we moved down the highway.

I've always had a special place in my heart for horses. As we drove along I found myself frequently glancing over at that tail blowing in the wind. Suddenly that tail caught the attention of every driver in the immediate vicinity. It stiffened and seemed almost to defy gravity as it arced upwards. The resulting explosion of fluid from beneath the tail nearly caused a major, multi-vehicle collision. While that fate was avoided, it did create a few moments of sheer highway bedlam.

The horse scored a direct hit on the grill, hood, windshield, and roof of the car immediately behind the trailer. The driver was trapped. If he swerved to the left he would have sideswiped my car. A swerve to the right would have had similar consequences with a transport truck. If he hit the brakes an armored truck would have made an unscheduled stop in his trunk. He took the full payload of the horse's bladder, although those of us in the immediate vicinity did suffer a few ricochet hits.

Steam rose from beneath the attacked car's hood. By the look on the driver's face the last time I saw it, before taking my opportunity to move ahead of the trailer, some of the horse fluid must have also gotten into the car's ventilation system. Clearly, he was in severe olfactory distress. Still, I can think of several things he should be thankful for, despite the particularly bad bit of luck showering down on him.

Can you imagine how he would have felt if he had left his sunroof open?

Despite the obvious reasons for being glad the event didn't result in a serious traffic accident, I wonder how he would have explained it all to the police, the emergency room staff, or his insurance agent.

I speak from experience. There are few things worse than a police officer suddenly seeing the humor in an accident in which you have been involved.

Since I had escaped the bombardment relatively unscathed, I was able to laugh about it. In fact, I laughed for about the next twenty miles. I laughed again when it brought back a memory from my childhood that had all but been erased in the nearly forty years that have passed.

I witnessed a similar event at the Canadian National Exhibition in Toronto. My brother stood just a little too close to the end of the horse that doesn't contain teeth when it let fly with a similar volley. The result was a significantly shortened day at the Exhibition, and a rather aromatically unpleasant streetcar trip home on a hot August day.

All of this, of course, brings the full meaning to 'Caution Horses'. Standing or driving within range of the north side of a horse when it's facing south is quite simply courting disaster. I know what I will do the next time I see a horsetail blowing in the breeze behind a trailer bearing the words, 'Caution Horses', and I'd recommend you do the same.

Close the windows and shut the sunroof . . .

Tightly.

Oh, and just in case you're ever tempted — never stand behind a loaded horse.

Road safety is something that we should all be concerned about these days. I am probably more aware of what can go wrong on the roads than most people. I'm coming up on the twelfth anniversary of the accident that took away a considerable amount of my mobility and foiled any plans I might have had to launch a career as a tango instructor. Not that I had any plans like that, especially since I have never tangoed in the first place, but still, it was just one of the many options that disappeared along with the feeling in my toes.

There has been a lot of discussion in the media lately about the safety issues of using cellular telephones while driving. Several jurisdictions are already, or are considering, implementing laws against the practice. The concern is apparently based on the concept that talking on a cellular phone distracts the driver.

I'm all for eliminating driver distractions. A man who felt it was more important to find a cassette tape on the floor of his car than it was to watch where he was going while driving caused the aforementioned lack of feeling in my toes. Therefore, perhaps we should ban listening to cassette tapes while driving. Naturally, that goes for compact disks, as well. Drivers with 8-track players in their pick-up trucks would be exempt, as long as they promise not to leave Alabama.

Let's take the whole stereo out of the car while we are at it. The radio can be just as distracting. Open line shows, political opinion disseminators, and any station playing those groups who have only learned two chords on their guitars are enough to drive anyone to distraction.

If cellular phones and car stereos have to go to help eliminate driver distraction, what about the greatest distraction of them all? Perhaps we should ban passengers. It might be necessary to phase that ban into practice. First, we could ban parents from driving with more than one child in the car. How many times have parents had difficulty concentrating on the road ahead while trying to break up a bad case of sibling rivalry in the back seat? I've often said that putting two teenage siblings too close together in the back of a vehicle can cause a meltdown of Chernobyl proportions. That's how we came to use the term 'nuclear family'.

Anyone ever convicted of backseat driving under the influence should be banned from riding in a vehicle for life. This is especially true of the ones who are under the influence of an over-inflated opinion of how much better a driver they are compared to the person whose hands are actually gripping the steering wheel.

We might have to ban drinking coffee while driving, too. Holding the steering wheel with one hand and a paper cup filled with a liquid just slightly cooler than the surface of the sun can be distracting on a number of levels. Level one is, "I hope I can hold this cup without spilling it on my lap." Level two is, "I hope I can get this cup up to my mouth without spilling it on my lap." Level three is, "I hope I don't scald my mouth with the coffee causing me to spill the cup on my lap." Level four is, "Yes, Officer, that's when I spilled my coffee on my lap."

I think it might be important to eliminate the windows in motor vehicles to further reduce driver distraction. Drivers shouldn't be reading signs and billboards while they are driving. The same goes for trying to read the fine print on another driver's bumper sticker. Removing the windows would definitely remove the distraction component from a roadside hazard near my place. We have a local woman who goes biking topless. She's been responsible for a number of distraction-related accidents that could have been eliminated if there weren't windows in cars. Perhaps drivers could be issued with periscopes so that they can see still see when they are about to run over a little old lady in a crosswalk.

All of the seats in cars should be converted to toilets, because, let's face it, there is nothing quite so distracting as looking for a rest stop when you really, really have to go.

I realize that I am advocating a complete removal of any and all distractions along the highways and byways of the continent, and that it might be a bit controversial stand to take. If you'd like to discuss it, call me in my car. I'm going out to see if that woman is on her bike today.

You can learn a lot about driving by observing other drivers. I had to be particularly aware of that while my youngest son went through driver training.

When I wrote my first driving test, I missed getting a perfect score by just one question. My father wondered what I could possibly have gotten wrong. When I told him it was the one that asked what you do when approaching a yellow light, he was even more confused. After all, doesn't everyone know what a yellow light means? How could his son have gotten that question wrong?

I tried to defend myself by pointing out that it was a multiple-choice question and there were several answers that might have been right. I could have chosen, "Stop no matter what," "Step on the gas and go through the intersection," "Stop if safe to do so," or, "Proceed with extreme caution." I told my father that I had taken answer b, "Step on the gas and go through the intersection."

"Where on earth did you get an idea like that," he shouted.

"From watching you, Dad," I replied.

My father was, to say the least, nonplussed. It had a regrettable impact on him. For the rest of his life, every time my father went through a yellow light, my mother would say, "That's right, Dear. Just step on the gas and go through . . . "

It would have been fine if we could have buried that little phrase with my parents, but my wife often witnessed my mother's little joke. She has carried it on throughout our thirty years of marriage. Every time I go through a yellow light I hear, "Yep. Just like your father. Step on the gas and go through . . . "

It's almost as annoying for me as it was for my father. I may have to take some desperate measures. If a light turns yellow I could hit the brakes hard and fast. I'm sure after a few near-lynchings by the shoulder belt, my wife might start begging me to step on the gas and go through.

It's only natural that we learn by observing. Over the years I've learned quite a few rules of the road just by watching how other drivers behave. For example:

Always drive in the passing lane, even if you only plan to drive at 70 percent of the posted speed limit. Never let drivers who might actually want to drive at the speed limit get past you, because you got there first.

If you put one of those chrome fish on the back of your car, you never have to let anyone merge in front of you. Of the six drivers who refused to let me merge in traffic one day last week, five of them had chrome fish on their trunks.

If you drive a car licensed in Tennessee or Alberta, the only reason your turn signal might be on is if it was that way when you bought the car.

Yield signs are only for the faint of heart.

One-way and stop signs in parking lots are only suggestions for other people to follow.

Canadian drivers over the age of sixty-five, when in the United States, will drive at the posted limit, but, since their speedometers are metric, they will drive in kilometers per hour not miles per hour. Therefore, a Canadian will be only be driving thirty miles an hour in a fifty zone.

American drivers of any age, when driving in Canada and seeing the metric speed sign indicating one hundred, will not convert it to approximately sixty miles per hour, but will simply assume that Canadians really like to drive fast.

There is a direct correlation between the amount of rust found on a pickup truck and the likelihood that it has a gun rack. Likewise, there is a direct correlation between the size of the tires on said pickup truck and the size and number of the pit bulls chained in the back.

If you drive a motor home on a winding two-lane mountain highway, you should never drive faster than 66 percent of the posted speed limit, and you should never pull over to let the other drivers pass.

If you drive with your high beams on at all times the other drivers will always be able to see you. They may be blinded and unable to see anything after you go by, but that's not your concern.

I've come up with a really great way to let the people like the ones in these examples know exactly what I think of them . . .

. . . but my family won't let me install a PA system in my car.

Over twenty-five years after the fact, I was invited to return to the scene of the crime. You'd think in all that time they might have forgotten by now.

My old high school asked me to come to speak to their Writer's Craft classes.

I had to wonder, do they really want me to come back to the school to talk to the students, or is it just some cunning sting operation to get me back to serve some outstanding detentions from 1972? The unserved sentence probably had something to do with the last day of school, a ten-pound box of Ivory Snow laundry soap, and the school fountain.

Looking back, high school was a lot of fun, interrupted by the requirement to attend certain classes. Some people, including most of the teachers, seemed to think that those classes were the primary purpose for going into the building each day. There was a belief that we were constantly learning things that would be used in our daily adult lives and make us more rounded individuals.

Math was a subject that I grudgingly accepted as a necessity for graduation, but could not predict any useful purpose for in my future. I was right. In the years since I left those hallowed halls, the Pythagorean theorem has not once come up in social conversation, nor has it ever served me any useful purpose in any of my career choices. You can imagine my dismay over the long hours I wasted studying for math exams, when just a couple years after I graduated, pocket calculators hit the market.

I plea-bargained my way through French. I was given a passing mark in my second last year on the condition that I not darken the doors of a French class in my final year. It was a deal that worked well for both parties. I got out of taking French and the teachers didn't have to listen to me trying to conjugate.

I can honestly say that I learned something important in chemistry. Ever since that explosion in the lab when I was in grade twelve I've avoided dropping lumps of phosphorous into beakers full of boiling sulfuric acid. I also learned to look closely for decimal places, because the explosion wouldn't have been nearly so spectacular if I had seen that I was to add "0.5 grams" of phosphorous. Adding 5 grams certainly accelerated and intensified the reaction the teacher told us to expect. I think it may have accelerated and intensified the change of the teacher's hair colour, as well.

I enjoyed geography, but with all the changes to the world map in the past many years it would appear that it was pretty much a waste of time. There isn't much practical purpose for knowing that Salisbury is the capital of Rhodesia when neither of them goes by that name anymore, and I can't tell you what has replaced them.

There was one English teacher who stood out — Mrs. Pat Cole. Of all the teachers I came in contact with over my years at Oakridge Secondary School, she is the reason I am writing today. Unlike the other English teachers I encountered, people who seemed to have been born, raised, and permanently mired in the 19th century, she showed me that there were good writers who weren't even dead yet. She took me to meet writers just starting out on their careers, men and women whose names were anything but household words, but who had stories to tell, and were willing to bring those stories out on cold winter nights to half empty library auditoriums. Some of them went on to fame and fortune — Margaret Atwood (*The Robber Bride* and many others) and Michael Ondaatje (*The English Patient* and many others) — while others drifted into obscurity, but every one of them taught me the importance of being a storyteller.

It was interesting returning to my old school. I was a bit disappointed to discover that they no longer have a fountain, so I guess I didn't need to bring a box of Ivory Snow after all.

Generally, I like birds. Some of them are beautiful, and others are just downright tasty.

I have, over the last little while, had a couple of run-ins with birds that have not left me thinking about how beautiful or tasty they might be.

Last week, I was working at my computer, minding my own business, when a bird decided to cause mass confusion, destruction, and a particularly sharp pain in my upper lap area.

I should point out that my office looks like a tornado has touched down inside it. I have piles of paper, enough to jumpstart a community recycling program, on my desk, in piles on the floor, and on my bookcases. There are also stacks of computer disks that will someday make their way into a storage box, but for now they are piled about twenty-five deep in several spots on my desk.

There's also my cat. Actually, it was my oldest son, Mike's, cat, but since he moved out to go to college, the feline equivalent of a paperweight has adopted me. This cat has two speeds, sound asleep, and slightly faster than a garden snail. She regularly gets me to lift her onto my windowsill, because getting there herself would take far too much energy. That's where she was when the bird caused all the problems.

The cat was sitting, peacefully looking out the window, waiting to fall asleep for the 312th time that day. A crow spotted her and decided to attack. Unfortunately, crows have a bit of difficulty understanding the concept of glass. The bird hit the window right beside the cat. This of course set off the chain reaction that left me sitting in even more disarray than usual and trying to alleviate that sharp pain I mentioned earlier.

When the bird hit the window, that cat went straight up, faster than I have seen her move in her entire life. Her landing was almost as ungraceful as the crow's. She missed the windowsill and came down on my desk, spreading paper, computer disks, paper clips, and whatever else got in her way from one end of the room to the other. She also dumped a freshly-poured cup of coffee onto my lap, thus causing the aforementioned pain.

Another recent bird encounter nearly caused a traffic accident.

I realize that my American readers revere the bald eagle for its majestic beauty. Normally, I enjoy watching an eagle soar, and there are hundreds of them that reside in my immediate vicinity. On this instance, however, I did not revere the eagles in question. In fact, I referred to them in a way that may very well be illegal in the United States. Luckily for me, it happened about a mile north of the border.

I was driving north from the border when I spotted three huge eagles sharing the same tree limb over the road. It was an incredible sight to see them watching the traffic pass below. It turns out they wanted to do something more than just watch the traffic. As I passed beneath their limb, they launched the eagle equivalent of a cruise missile at my windshield. Two of the birds made a direct hit.

Two massive deposits of bird crap, each the size of a dinner plate, obscured my vision. I immediately hit my windshield washer button. In case you're wondering, windshield wiper fluid might remove a sparrow's deposit, but it sure doesn't do anything for eagle crap. The blue washer fluid, when mixed with the whitish deposit, created an opaque turquoise mess across the entire windshield. I was, for all intents and purposes, driving blind.

I managed to get the car stopped without putting it into a ditch, hitting a tree, or running over anyone. The washer fluid and bird crap mixture looked like glue. As the alcohol evaporated from the washer fluid, it started to harden into a solid mass that smelled like fermented rotten fish. The windshield wipers were having a difficult time moving. I, on the other hand, was not having a difficult time coming up with numerous adjectives for eagles that Audubon never thought of.

It took a good twenty minutes to scrape enough of the foul fowl mixture off the windshield to continue driving. I had to drive through a car wash four times before the last remnants of eagle dung disappeared. I probably could have gotten it off with one or two washes, but the first one included hot carnauba wax, which just gave the stuff a nice shiny gleam.

While I wouldn't wish any harm to these majestic birds, I wouldn't mind if they were to get really, really constipated.

Christmas always seems to be a time when we are filled with expectations that never seem to get fully met. That box under the tree with your name on it might be just the right size for a gift you want more than anything else. You might as easily discover on Christmas morning that the box is also the right size for a pair of socks, a hideous tie, or the same book you got last year . . . and the year before . . .

I always go into the season expecting it to go smoothly. I realize that I should know better. If there is one thing that the Christmas season is notorious for, it's that it rarely, if ever, goes smoothly. In other years we've faced a variety of Yuletide disasters. One year we had no water. Another year we had no electricity. There was the year that the turkey was so tough it broke the blade of my carving knife.

I should have expected that this Christmas season would be preordained to bring forth another unexpected calamity. Of course, one person's calamity can be another person's good fortune. This year's calamities have made sure that my mechanic will have a good Christmas. In the past three weeks, we've been very generous to him, or rather, our cars have been very generous to him. Between my wife and I, we've spent over $3,000 in car repairs since the first of December.

Diane's car needed a new battery, a new alternator, and a new transmission thingamajig — all on separate visits to the shop. My car needed a new $400 seat bracket in between Diane's alternator and her transmission thingamajig.

The day after we wrote a check for over $1,000 for work on Diane's car, mine became flatulent. I've never known a car to become flatulent before, but there I was, driving along, minding my own business, when the car let loose with an aroma that even my dog couldn't top after eating a can of deep brown beans. It was vile. I've hit skunks that smelled better than whatever was coming from under my hood.

"Where are they?" I demanded to know when I walked into my mechanic's shop the next morning.

"Where are what?" he said, obviously pretending that he had no idea what I was talking about.

"The voodoo dolls," I said. "I want to see the voodoo dolls shaped like my cars that you've been sticking pins into all month.

Despite his denials, I'm convinced he's been using some kind of black magic on my cars. What other explanation can there be for a total of six trips to the shop in less than three weeks. This last one was the killer. Apparently, my car's flatulence was caused by the compressor clutch giving up the ghost. A new compressor clutch cost me one thousand, two hundred and thirty eight dollars and four cents.

Of course, this sort of thing couldn't happen in a month like March when there aren't other ways to go through that kind of money. The cars had been running smoothly through the inexpensive months like July and

October. It wasn't until I had gone Christmas shopping that the cars decided to attack my bank account. In a way, that's a good thing, because it would have been The Clutch That Stole Christmas if I hadn't already spent the Christmas money. On Christmas morning, we might have all gathered around my new compressor or Diane's new alternator. We could have wrapped up the bills for the new seat bracket or the transmission thingamajig.

Despite this year's Christmas calamities, it's still the season to be jolly. I'm sure my mechanic is feeling quite jolly, and I wouldn't want to take that away from him. But if one more thing goes wrong with either of our cars, I'm going to tell him to fa la la la la la la la la.

I've given up trying to remember what day it is. I just follow my schedule. If I was in Toronto yesterday, I must be in Ottawa today. Forget Tuesday, Wednesday, and all that; these days my days of the week get named after a new city.

Over the next few weeks my days are going to be called everything from Birmingham, Alabama to Red Deer, Alberta. I'm working at beating my old record of five nights in hotel rooms in different cities with the same painting on the walls. In there somewhere I also have to get my column written each week.

Anyone who thinks being a writer on a book tour is some sort of glamorous activity, never had to be in fifteen different cities on fifteen consecutive nights. Life on the road is definitely a unique experience. Sometimes it's even interesting, and if enough people come out to see me, or if the media gets interested, it can even be ego boosting. Glamorous though . . . ? No. I feel like I'm being dragged from one end of the country to the other and put on display like a circus performer.

A typical book tour involves visiting bookstores, newspapers, radio stations, and TV studios. Each evening I end up in a bookstore, reading selections from the book, signing copies for the customers, and falling into whatever bed I'm calling home that night. The next morning I get to start all over again . . . and again . . . and again, through over sixty cities from one corner of the continent to the other.

The best part of the whole thing is meeting the people who read the column, or who have picked up the book. The number that show up each night is largely determined by a number of factors. Sunny warm evenings, people have lots of better things to do with their time. Rainy evenings, they might decide to come and see me. How a bookstore promotes the event can have a pretty major impact as well. In a suburb of Toronto last week, the store staff had only read part of the material sent to them about the book. They somehow came to the conclusion that I had written a book about using humor to deal with stress. As a result, a couple of psychiatric nurses showed up for the event, but left when they discovered the truth about my book.

Interacting with the audience members is always a lot of fun. When I did a few appearances in Texas a couple of years ago, I told the audience that the reason I walk on crutches is I broke my spine in a serious golfing accident. Before I could explain that I had been in a car accident on my way to the golf course, a Texan in the audience slowly drawled, "Y'all play a deff'rent kinda game up there in Canada . . . Kinda like hockey where ya get to beat the crap out of th'other players?"

Sometimes you get to visit places you remember from your childhood. I've now learned that it might not be a really good idea to go looking for them. Last night I found myself near the place where my father spent his childhood in the 1920s. I found the farmhouse where he and his mother lived after his father died. It's still a working farm, but the city has pushed out. Suburban subdivisions have appeared right beside the farm. His uncle's farmhouse is still across the road, but Ottawa's NHL arena stands where the cows once grazed. The one-room schoolhouse where my grandmother taught has disappeared and been replaced with a mini-mart. I went looking for the old graveyard that was filled with relatives of mine from the 19th century. Houses now stand there. Between two I spotted a couple of headstones looking more like landscaping than memorials. I would have had to walk through backyards to find my great-grandparent's final resting places. Obviously these homeowners never saw *Poltergeist I, II* or *III*.

For the next few months, I'll be filing my columns from the road. No doubt, I'll see a lot of the people who read it each week, and I'll probably also see enough identical hotel rooms and bookstores to start believing in deja vu all over again. I'll squeeze myself into airline seats and small rental cars; none of which ever seem to be designed for people remotely my size. I'll eat burgers on the run between TV studios and bookstores, and learn to enjoy stomach tablets for dessert. I'll wander around in a daze trying to remember what day, city or time zone I'm supposed to be in.

It might not be glamorous, but it sure is fun.

I've spent the last few days in Louisville, Kentucky. It seems there are a number of distinct ways to pronounce the name of this city. According to the card included with my registration package for the National Society of Newspaper Columnists Convention it is acceptable to say:

Looavull

Luhvul

Lewisville

Looaville

Looeyville.

Apparently, no matter how you say it to a local, you will be wrong. As a husband and father I'm pretty much used to being wrong a lot of the time anyway.

The National Society of Newspaper Columnists was supposedly established over twenty years ago to further the development of columnists and column writing. This development takes place while we listen to Pulitzer Prize nominees and winners tell us why they are and we aren't, visit the bar fridge in the hospitality suite, talk with our peers about the trials and tribulations we face getting a regular column written, revisit the hospitality suite, experience the sights, sounds, and tastes of another columnist's home city, and, of course, spend more time drinking in the hospitality suite.

In keeping with the need to experience the host city, we all boarded busses and headed off to Churchill Downs, home of the famed Kentucky Derby Horse Race. Our professional development continued at the track while we tried to place bets on the races, and consume even more of the local tastes. Most of us stuck to tasting bourbon and mint juleps. As the afternoon wore on, because of the heat and humidity, our thirsts needed frequent quenching. This, of course, made concentrating on picking logical winners slightly more difficult. I think the powers that be at Churchill Downs were somehow banking on our cognitive abilities reducing as our thirst needed additional glasses of bourbon or mint juleps. They seemed quite happy to see us placing bets on horses based on their neat-sounding names instead of wasting time checking to see if the animal had ever come close to winning a race.

The first race featured a horse called American Press. Naturally, this seemed like an omen for all the columnists — a horse to represent us all at the winner's circle. Bets were made. The excitement grew. The horses paraded to the post. They entered the gate. The bell rang, and ten horses started to run. American Press ran like it was looking forward to a career in the adhesive industry. Perhaps, someday soon, it will find itself in a bottle of glue in the advertising paste-up department of a newspaper near you.

Naturally, this setback required more bourbon and mint juleps to ease the sense of loss we were all feeling.

I don't even want to talk about the second race.

How could I pass up betting on a horse called Trip in the third? Trip is something I do quite well. I'm proud of my record of never once missing the ground when I've tripped.

Trip was not a fast horse. The ambulance that drives around the track well behind the race nearly beat him.

By the fifth race, I figured out what some of those numbers meant beside the horses' names. I had been neglecting the odds, the horses' winning records, and a whole bunch of other statistics. Perhaps I'm better able to get in touch with the logical part of my brain after a couple of bourbons. I bet on what appeared to be the favorite. I'm pleased to say I won my bet. I pocketed the substantial sum of $2.20 in return for the $2.00 bet.

The National Association of Newspaper Columnists sponsored the sixth race. I won the right to be part of the group that presented the trophy to the winning horse. I even bet on the winner, a fine animal that went by the name Flattened.

That seemed like a fitting name for me to bet on. I've been flattened in three car accidents and, after such copious amounts of bourbon, I think my brainwaves had been somewhat flattened. Surprisingly, Flattened won the race and paid enough to erase all of my earlier losing wagers. Obviously, this was a horse to be proud of. If I was its owner, I would have been ecstatic.

But Flattened's owner wasn't all that excited. He immediately sold the horse, and left us all with a quote about his feelings for noble beast. It was the kind of quote that every newspaper columnist dreams of getting.

"I just hope she doesn't come back and bite me on the ass in the future."

I think that's what the bourbon did to me the next morning.

Like most people who live north of, and rarely venture south of the Mason-Dixon line, I had some preconceived notions about what it would be like to be 'way down south in Dixie'. These concepts were fostered by television shows like Andy Griffith, Gomer Pyle, and Green Acres.

I will readily admit that I expected to meet a bunch of people whose names were Bubba, Daisy-Mae, and Billy-Joe-Ray-Bob.

Television news is also responsible for creating and maintaining the image many of us have of the South. They seem to be able to find unique, stereotypical southern goobers to interview whenever a natural or manmade disaster takes place down here. One could almost believe that, aside from leveling houses, tornadoes always remove the teeth of the people left behind to be interviewed by the news crews.

Most of the radio and TV interviews I've done on this trip have, at some point, gotten around to the question about what I have found different than I expected down here. The first thing that comes to my mind is that I expected it to be a lot drier. Oh sure, I expected it to be humid, but the humidity has been falling from the sky in rather surprising amounts.

On one of the days I spent in Atlanta over five inches of humidity fell. On the first morning I spent in Birmingham, Alabama, it rained so hard I was wetter stepping out of my car than I was when I stepped out of the shower.

True to form, the TV news that night featured a story about a man who fits our preconceived notions about Southerners. He had been driving in the storm and became trapped when he tried to drive through a washed-out highway underpass. Rescue crews got him safely back on dry land.

I had to check with members of my audience that night to be sure that what I saw next actually occurred. Several audience members assured me that I wasn't mistaken. The rescue crews also brought the man's seeing-eye dog to safety. No wonder he didn't see the big puddle.

One audience member summed it up for us all when he said, "I never knew them dawgs could drive."

At least now I know why drive-up automatic bank machines have Braille on the buttons.

Most of the people I've met on this tour through the Deep South have been pretty much the same sort of folks you'll find anywhere else in the country, except they all seem to think I talk funny, or rather "tawk funnai." I, on the other hand, have a somewhat similar opinion about their linguistic nuances. For example, I very nearly got into a lot of trouble in Huntsville, Alabama when a waitress offered me a piece of ass for my Coke. I thought it sounded like a pretty good trade, but it turned out she meant a cube of frozen water when she said "ass." Just as well, my wife was with me and I might not have survived the consequences.

I, also, use several words that are not immediately understood down here. It's taken me most of the trip to stop referring to that special little room we all need to visit fairly frequently by its Canadian name. I get a blank stare when I ask directions to "the washroom." I'm supposed to ask for the bathroom or the restroom. I can't understand calling it by one of those names in a gas station. I have no intention of taking a bath or a rest in there, but I will be washing at some point in the visit.

My wife really confused a waitress in Louisville when she asked for a bowl of porridge for breakfast. In a grocery store she asked a clerk to direct her to the aisle where they kept the pop. After an extended blank stare, the clerk asked her if she was talking about 'soda'. Diane thought he meant baking soda and said, "No, the pop, like Coke or Pepsi." The clerk walked away talking to himself about dumb Northerners.

Truth be known, we have really enjoyed all of the people we met down here in Dixie. I can't recall being around so many friendly people. Friendly, that is, when you are talking to them on the street or in a store or restaurant. When they get behind the wheel of their cars and pickup trucks it seems their friendliness gets put in the trunk or the cargo box.

Merge seems to have a different meaning down here. People seem to think it's a full contact sport. Instead of referring to the process of allowing two lanes of traffic to flow smoothly into one lane, it means prevent the other guy from moving over at all costs. Turn signals only seem to operate if they were turned on when the person bought the vehicle.

I was asked after one of my appearances if I thought I would want to tour the South again. Y'all are darn tootin' I'd do it again . . .

. . . in a New York minute.

I guess none of us really think we speak with any kind of an accent. It's always the other guy who "tawks funnai." My Canadian tongue spits out certain words that readily identify me as someone who 'ain't from around these parts, are y'all?' In particular, my pronunciation of 'out', 'about', and 'house' sound peculiar when they are heard by Tennesseean ears. This became abundantly clear when a radio host in Nashville kept asking me to say 'house'. I really confused him when I said, "There's a mouse out and about the house . . . y'all"

Getting lost in Tennessee is not something that I would recommend. Asking directions can leave you almost as confused as you were before you started. I asked a waitress how to find West End Avenue in Nashville. She spoke for nearly five minutes about how terrible she is at giving directions . . . at least that's what I think she was telling me. Several times I could have sworn she mentioned Florida and Georgia, which really confused me. I didn't think I would have to cross two state lines just to get to another section of Nashville.

There was one Tennessee experience I really didn't want to miss. I've often looked at the magazine ads for Jack Daniels Tennessee Whisky. They always include an invitation to drop by the distillery if you're ever in the area. I thought it might be fun to take them up on the invitation so I found Lynchburg, Tennessee on my road map. It appeared to be a little over an hour from our hotel. My wife and I set out early in the morning, expecting to get there before the temperature and humidity made it too uncomfortable for our northern bodies to cope.

We were fine until we hit Shelbyville, which by our calculations was only about fifteen minutes from our date with some of Uncle Jack's sippin' whisky. It probably would have been only fifteen minutes if the local government in Shelbyville hadn't chosen that same weekend to tear up the roads. A few dollars in the budget for detour route signs might have been nice. Finally, after getting lost west of town, and again north of town, we had no choice. We had to stop and ask a man for directions.

Listening to that man talk only served to make me realize that I should have invested in an English/Tennesseean dictionary. We eventually got the idea of what he was saying, even though the only words we were absolutely sure of during the ten-minute disser- tation were, "Y'all have a nice day now, y'hear." I think at one point he told us to make a left turn at the corner where the red barn burnt down back in '57.

In the end our drive to Lynchburg took us over two hours. We pulled into the parking lot ready to take the tour, because we knew from taking similar tours that it was a prerequisite to getting the free samples. We watched a movie that had English subtitles for those who didn't understand the Tennesseean. We learned that the water they use has no "arn" (iron) in it. We also learned about the importance of filtering the whisky through ten feet of charcoal to make it "meller" (mellow.) Watching the film made me that much more anxious to get a sample of the product.

While the others in the tour headed off to see the process first hand, my wife and I decided that climbing a total of over 100 stairs was not something I wanted to do on crutches with the temperature over 100 degrees. We were led to the hospitality room.

At long last, we were going to get some southern hospitality and a big old glass of Jack Daniels on the rocks. I was so hot that I planned on taking a couple of the ice cubes and dropping them down my shorts.

That's when we learned the horrible truth. There would be no free samples of Jack Daniels. Lynchburg, Tennessee is located in a county that has outlawed the distribution of alcohol since 1909. All they serve is lemonade. Okay, so it was pretty good lemonade, but when you're expecting to let a free sample of Jack Daniels slide down your throat lemonade just doesn't cut it. Besides, I reasoned that ice cubes from a glass of lemonade would probably be stickier than I was, so I couldn't drop them down my shorts.

I was so upset I could have written a country song with a title like, "My Heart Done Got Broked At The Jack Daniels Bar With Nothin' To Drink But Lemonade". Of course, I realize that it wouldn't sell that well because I couldn't figure out how to get in a verse about a pickup truck, a dog, and a cheatin', mistreatin' set of twins.

It just goes to show how wrong clichés can be. They might make it in Lynchburg, but not even an itty-bitty sample of the best thing in life is free there.

Two roadside motels that I've ended up staying in, for no other reason than they were the first ones I found with vacancies when I was too tired to drive any further, have shown me both ends of the travel experience spectrum.

A few years ago I stopped at a small hotel about 250 miles from home. I was in cattle ranching country, so it didn't surprise me to see that the hotel had a western motif. The sign outside advertised the room rate, which included breakfast the next morning featuring, "Good Country Style Home Cookin'".

I stepped into the lobby, which featured a large stone fireplace. The walls displayed a variety of heads that used to be attached to live deer, moose, bears, longhorn cattle, and mountain lions. The staff wore jeans, cowboy boots, Stetsons, and shirts that looked like they had come from the wardrobe department of a 1950s singing cowboy movie. One even sported a finely tooled leather holster around his waist. Instead of a gun it sported a squirt gun full of blue window cleaner.

The whole scene looked truly authentic, except for one minor factor. Every single member of the staff was a recent immigrant from the Indian Subcontinent. The owner played the juxtaposition of cultures to its fullest.

He was well aware of the comedic value of the whole scene.

He looked up from his work when I approached the desk and said, "Howdy, Partner," in his thick East Indian accent. His face broke into a broad grin, and he immediately began to laugh in a deep, infectious manner that welcomed me to share his joke.

The next morning I took them up on the free breakfast. It featured some of the best "country style home cookin'" I've run into anywhere. Given the chance, I'd stay there again.

The other experience occurred more recently. I decided not to bother returning home from Seattle after a meeting I was attending ran longer than usual. I started looking for a place to stay at the south end of the city and didn't find one until I had gone thirty miles north of the city. Apparently several thousand Jehovah's Witnesses had hit town for a convention. I moved from place to place finding no room at the inns.

I ended up in a motel that is part of a national chain of inexpensive roadside motels. I was exhausted by the time I got to my room, so I went straight to bed. A discovery I made in the morning made me wish I had spent a bit more time looking around the room before turning in.

I stepped out of the shower and reached for a towel. On the shelf beside the bath towels I spotted a condom left behind by a previous user of the room. I chose to dry myself with the hand towel from the ring beside the sink, because, well, let's just say that the condom was not in its original packaging.

I don't like complaining. I hate returning purchases to a store. Somehow, though, I thought that finding a condom on the towel shelf was the sort of thing that warranted a little deeply-felt complaining. At the very least, I thought the chain's head office would be concerned about their staff leaving an item like that for the next guest to find.

They were.

They were so concerned they sent me a form letter.

It contained the usual corporate bovine excrement. It said their company "strives to adhere to a high standard of quality and service throughout all of our properties nationwide." One statement that did ring true, though, was, " . . . we are committed to providing legendary service to our guests." Believe me, finding a previous guest's condom in your room is definitely ranks right up there on the legendary scale.

Maybe I should have expected to make that kind of discovery in my room. I may have been mispronouncing the name of the motel chain. I thought its name had a number in it, but one might expect to find a secondhand condom if it was called Motel Sex.

Brings a whole new meaning to the term 'hotel safe' doesn't it?

Here I go again, doing something that I know will lead to discomfort, unpleasantness and a general lack of sleep. Once a year I put myself in this situation to attend a convention on a topic about which I know the dark side of sweet diddlysquat, but it's something my wife enjoys doing.

When Diane accompanies me to a convention she has to put up with the indignities of luxury hotel suites, poolside bar service, fine dining, and comfort. When I accompany her to this convention I get to camp.

This is not even camping in the sense normal people might expect to do it. We won't be in a traditional campground with leveled sites, picnic tables, and a fully-stocked general store. There won't be any electrical hook-ups. There are no showers. There is no running water. In fact, there is no water at all. The place is a virtual desert. We have to bring in our own supply of water for the event. I don't even want to talk about the sanitary facilities. Believe me, you don't want to read about them either.

The event takes place 7,500 feet above sea level, on top of a mountain with several hundred amateur astronomers — Diane included. The location is perfect for the astronomically enthused. There are no city lights to blot out the stars. The view covers almost the entire sky, without trees or other mountains in the way. There is ample room for them all to set up their telescopes and look into the night sky in search of the rings around Uranus.

I am not a "good camper". Camping to me means staying alive when there are no hotel rooms to be found.

I don't like the taste of dust in my coffee. I like to know that when I feel the need to seek out the sanitary facilities, I won't be sharing the cubicle with a variety of spiders, wasps, and hepatitis germs. I like to sleep in a bed at night. I don't like to think about the cougars and grizzly bears that consider my campsite their turf.

When I sleep away from home I want in-room coffee service, HBO, and free local calling. I need to know that at the end of the day, if I suddenly feel the need for sustenance, I can get a pizza delivered within half an hour. I know that when I stop by a hotel bar they aren't going to say, "We're sorry sir, but all the ice melted in our cooler yesterday so you'll have to drink your beer warm."

None of that is available when I camp — especially when I have to camp on top of a barren mountain.

Camping with amateur astronomers has its own special delights. Naturally, these people don't sleep at night. They spend the darkened hours peering into the sky. It's like being the only mortal at a vampire's convention. For those of us who are not astronomically excitable — basically the husbands and wives of the people who are — there is no good time for us to sleep. The night is filled with the sounds of people shouting about their latest stellar discovery. The day is filled with the sounds of snoring from every campsite.

You can't even carry a normal flashlight around these people. White light does to an astronomer what daylight does to a vampire. If you turn on a flashlight to ensure your safety on the way to the unsanitary facilities, you will incur the wrath of every stargazer on the mountain. For some reason, which I don't fully understand, red lights do not bother them. I guess it's like shooting a werewolf with a bullet that isn't made of silver.

Unfortunately, red flashlights don't always provide enough light to ensure you make it to the unsanitary facilities without tripping over a grizzly bear.

Chances are the trip will work out fine. I may not sit on a black widow spider in one of the portable outhouses. There are reasonably good odds that a cougar won't drag me off if I fall asleep trying to sound interested in whatever it is my wife is looking at through her telescope. There's at least a fifty-fifty chance that I will make it through the entire five days without major emotional scars due to the lack of TV, radio, newspapers, or my computer. I might even enjoy being away from all that, and the telephone, too.

Still, if you look up tonight and see the first faint star, I'd be grateful if you make a little wish that I don't trip over any grizzly bears.

And after the event . . .

The fact that I survived last weekend without tripping over a grizzly bear or being dragged off by a cougar should not be interpreted as an indication that I had a good time on top of Table Mountain with several hundred astronomers. I had a spectacularly miserable time. I firmly believe that the only reason I didn't run afoul of grizzly bears or cougars is that it was just too freaking cold for them to venture out of their warm dens, thus proving that they are smarter than the average astronomer.

At this same event last summer we roasted under a blazing sun. Daytime temperatures reached egg-frying levels. This weekend it rained, the wind blew, and several times it came very close to snow. When I got out of the tent on Sunday morning the temperature was hovering imperceptibly above the freezing point. The wind-chill factor dropped it to well below freezing.

Until the experience of sleeping, or at least trying to sleep, in a tent in those kinds of temperatures, I hadn't realized that you could use shivering as an aerobic exercise.

There is no need for caffeine when you are on a mountaintop with the temperature hovering just above the freezing point. If sitting on a nearly frozen plastic outhouse toilet seat doesn't jar you into a full degree of consciousness, nothing will.

As I predicted, the public restrooms consisted of a few strategically placed portable outhouses. Twice a day a truck arrived to pump out the pits and hose down the entire structure with disinfectant. It wasn't frequent enough. I spent the whole weekend praying for constipation. Unfortunately, here was one of those cases that prove that not all prayers get answered satisfactorily.

Aside from the general unpleasantness of dealing with outhouses, I had to contend with the fact that these particular units were not designed with people my size in mind. I have often admitted that I am "big for my age." The cubic space available in the outhouses was just barely larger than the cubic space I occupy. Basically, the sum of my parts was almost greater than the airspace in the outhouse. Only with a great deal of effort was I able to prevent the astronomers from having a second moon to view through their telescopes. On more than one occasion I was afraid that my naked butt was going to be visible to several hundred naked eyes.

I don't even want to talk about the effects of sharing the mountaintop with toilet paper thieves. Suffice to say that it doesn't add any joy to the whole experience to find yourself literally freezing your butt on a toilet seat and having to wait for someone to come along and rescue you with a spare roll of tissue.

Cold, discomfort, annoyance, and fear of having to make another trip to the cocoon-like outhouses can make people's thought processes go a little wonky. My wife, and most of the other astronomically-enthused people on the mountain, thought all the discomfort was worthwhile because she got to see meteors, fireballs, galaxies, and nebulae.

I might have been more enthusiastic if one of the fireballs had landed near our tent. At least that would have given me a source of heat to thaw my butt with after a trip to the outhouse.